Edwin and John

"In the diary *Jeb and Dash*, where each person is given an identity that disguises him, there appears Little Nicky. In *Edwin and John*, we see Little Nicky as he really was and as he continued his life as John Zeigler."
                                                      Michael Conley, playwright

"Imagine yourself sitting down to dinner with a perfect host and listening to him tell a fascinating tale of two men in love and their adventures over nearly fifty years together. . . ."
               David Masello, essayist, Senior Editor at *Town and Country*

"How magnificently the poems capture the loving and sharing between the two men. They give their reader such a rare look at a life-altering, life-enriching, life-affirming relationship. I think they are very beautiful and the entire volume is a tasteful and lovely tribute to two fine men."
                                              Elaine Schwartz, poetry therapist

Edwin and John
A Personal History of the
American South

James T. Sears

LONDON AND NEW YORK

First published 2009
by Routledge

Published 2019 by Routledge
2 Park Square, Milton Park, Abingdon, Oxon OX14 4RN
52 Vanderbilt Avenue, New York, NY 10017

*Routledge is an imprint of the Taylor & Francis Group,
an informa business*

Copyright © 2009 James T. Sears

Typeset in Sabon by
Keystroke, 28 High Street, Tettenhall, Wolverhampton

All rights reserved. No part of this book may be reprinted or reproduced or utilized in any form or by any electronic, mechanical, or other means, now known or hereafter invented, including photocopying and recording, or in any information storage or retrieval system, without permission in writing from the publishers.

Notice:
Product or corporate names may be
trademarks or registered trademarks, and are used only for identification and explanation without intent to infringe.

Library of Congress Cataloging in Publication Data
Sears, James T. (James Thomas), 1951–
Edwin and John: A Personal History of the American
South / by James T. Sears.
p. cm.
Includes bibliographical references and index.
1. Peacock, Edwin, 1910–1989. 2. Ziegler, John, 1912– . Gay couples—United States—Biography. 4. Gay men—United States—Biography. 5. Homosexuality—United States. I. Title.
HQ75.7.S43 2009
306.76′62092275—dc22   2008034591

ISBN13: 978-1-56023-761-7 (pbk)
ISBN13: 978-0-203-88313-6 (ebk)

Contents

List of Illustrations vii
Foreword ix
Acknowledgments xi
About the Author xii
Introduction xiii

PART I
Early Years 1

1. Clingman's Dome 3
2. A Cure? 8
3. What Must One Do? 13
4. The Incident 19
5. Lean Wolf Hours 25

PART II
War Years 33

6. A Yeoman's Journey 35
7. Colorado Schooling 43
8. Yakutat 47
9. Cape Chiniak 62
10. Reunion 76
11. Edwin's Discharge 82
12. At Sea 86

PART III
Book Basement, Travels, and Beyond   99

13 The Book Basement Years   101

14 Last Years   115

Afterword: After Edwin   123
Notes   128
Index   139

Illustrations

All photographs are used with kind permission from the collection of John A. Zeigler, Jr.

I.1	Edwin and John, Sullivan's Island, 1947	xiv
I.2	Edwin and John, Christmas Eve, circa 1980s	xiv
I.3	James Sears overlooks John Zeigler as they review his World War II correspondence	xvi
1.1	John and Isham "Dash" Perkins circa 1950	4
1.2	Edwin at Smoky Mountains on trip to Clingman's Dome, 1940	6
2.1	Edwin with sister Virginia at family Thomasville home, 1919	11
3.1	John at Sullivan's Island, 1933	15
4.1	John at home out of Santa Fe, New Mexico, 1941	21
5.1	Phil Bell "Max," Carter "Jeb," and John "Little Nicky"	28
6.1	Edwin and John together in the Navy	41
8.1	John at Yakutat, Alaska	48
9.1	Edwin at Camp Chiniak, Alaska	71
10.1	George Scheirer and John in Washington, D.C.	78
13.1	Edwin and John at front of The Book Basement	102
13.2	Edwin shelving at The Book Basement	107
13.3	Edward N., John, Bob, Carson, Edwin, Reeves, Charleston, 1948	111
13.4	Carson, Edwin, and John, 1954, Charleston	113
13.5	The Book Basement. Etching by Prentiss Taylor	114
14.1	Edwin and John in Europe, circa late 1970s	118
14.2	Edwin looking down onto John, circa 1980s	122
15.1	John with actor John Clayton portraying him in a play by Michael Conley based on the book *Jeb and Dash*, 2005	124
15.2	Edwin and John at couple's screened porch, October 1972, Charleston	126

Foreword

Edwin died in 1989, a few months before what would have been our fiftieth anniversary. We had planned to celebrate at a friend's hotel in Eastbourne England, with our friends coming from many different countries.

Back then, there was rarely talk about gay marriage. I am sure that the consensus among friends our age or slightly younger would have been that we would prefer legal rights but didn't feel the need for marriage licenses to make our commitments last. None of us had to worry about visiting rights or wills.

The young Christian gay today is more interested in marriage than most of my friends, who are non-believers. But, I think gay marriage should be welcomed by anyone who believes in the sanctity of marriage or the questionable idea that marriage promotes fidelity.

I sometimes wonder what my friends in Washington during the 1930s would have thought about current gay possibilities and the sacrifices that have brought them about. Most of us worked for the government, where no questions were asked—until the McCarthy years, when several of my friends lost their jobs.

Jeb and Dash, excerpts from the diary of Carter Beeler edited by his niece Ina Russell, covers those years in Washington. When a friend insisted that I read the book, it took me many pages before I realized that I was reading about *my* closest friends and that I was "Little Nicky!" Ina, of course, wanted to protect the gay men in the diary and altered some of the facts besides changing names. There is also little sex in them. *Edwin and John* corrects these and other matters.

Now I am "Old John," who welcomes the advances in the acceptance of gays into the mainstream, though I and most of my friends never suffered the indignities many others have throughout their lives, especially in the American South.

John A. Zeigler, Jr.
Charleston, South Carolina

Acknowledgments

This book could never have been written without the insight and expertise of my friend, Jim Sears. I wish to thank him as well as Edwin's and my loving, supportive families and friends.

John A. Zeigler, Jr.

About the Author

James T. Sears specializes in research in lesbian, gay, bisexual, and transgender issues in education, curriculum studies, and history. He earned an undergraduate degree in history from Southern Illinois University, a graduate degree in political science from the University of Wisconsin, and his doctorate in education and sociology from Indiana University, which awarded him its Outstanding Alumni Award. Sears is the author or editor of eighteen books, including his groundbreaking *Growing Up Gay in the South* as well as *Lonely Hunters: An Oral History of Lesbian and Gay Southern Life* (A 1998 finalist for the American Library Association gay non-fiction award) and *Behind the Mask of the Mattachine* (finalist for the Lambda non-fiction Book Award). He has authored *The Encyclopedia of Sex, Courtship and Culture: The Twentieth and Twenty-First Centuries* and *Growing Older: The Millennial LGBTs*. Sears lectures throughout the world and has taught at Harvard University, Trinity University, Indiana University, Penn State University, the College of Charleston, and the University of South Carolina. He has also been a Research Fellow at the Center for Feminist Studies at the University of Southern California, a Fulbright Senior Research Southeast Asia Scholar on sexuality and culture, a Research Fellow at the University of Queensland and CNPq research lecturer in Brazil.

Introduction

This is a story of the remarkable fifty-year relationship between Edwin Peacock and John Zeigler, Jr. Edwin was born in Thomasville, Georgia in 1910; John was born in Manning, South Carolina two years later. *Edwin and John* is a Southern love story set against the backdrop of World War II and the post-war South, where they opened a bookshop in what was then the small town of Charleston. How these two men forged a relationship that endured the conflicts of war and emotion, openly shared their lives, and dealt with tragedy and death is Edwin and John's story.

This is also a tale of two boys growing up gay in the South during an era in which "gay" was simply an ordinary word and discussion of any type of sexuality was, at the very least, impolite. Edwin was raised in a large family. His father was a druggist, and his mother, born on her family's ante-bellum Greenwood Plantation, had moved to Thomasville at the turn of the century. While Edwin had few sexual experiences growing up, he knew his attractions were to men. He enjoyed the friendship of women, telling stories and pulling harmless pranks. His greatest childhood love, though, was botany. After graduating from high school and a couple of years working in his father's drugstore, the twenty-something Edwin moved to Columbus, Georgia for work in the Civilian Conservation Corps. It was there he met Carson Smith, an adolescent pianist who had suffered from rheumatic fever. The two formed a lifelong friendship as Edwin encouraged her writing interest. Carson would later fictionalize Edwin as the homosexual deaf-mute, John Singer, in her first novel, *The Heart is a Lonely Hunter*.

John's family moved from town to town before settling in Florence, South Carolina when he was five years old. His father also had been a druggist but soon began a newspaper, in which he editorialized against the Klan and venal Southern politicians. Although less outgoing than Edwin, John found more opportunities for same-sex relationships, including a lad who became his lifelong friend. John moved to Charleston to enter The Citadel in 1928, where he fell in love with poetry and with his second-year roommate. Their relationship resembled those found in

xiv *Introduction*

Figure I.1 Edwin and John, Sullivan's Island, 1947

Figure I.2 Edwin and John, Christmas Eve, circa 1980s

British boarding schools of the era as the two young men shared their love through literature and classical music, long walks along Charleston's Battery, and schoolboy intimacy. A couple of years after graduation, John moved to Washington, D.C. to work and eventually lodge with a group of other gay men.

In the edited diary *Jeb and Dash*, "Little Nicky" resides, separately, at a D.C. apartment house with three other gay men.[1] "I knew Carter ('Jeb') kept some kind of diary," John told me, "he always talked about it, but I had no idea it was so detailed until Ina, his niece, sent me a copy of several years from the original diary." In Ina Russell's version, youthful Nicky dies in World War II; in real life, John survives the war (spending much of it with Edwin) and then returns to Charleston where they live together. As the sole survivor of this group, John recounts the inside story of his years with "Jeb and Dash."

Approaching the age of 100, John today retains his keen intellect and vibrant spirit. His lifetime spans enormous change in social attitudes. *Edwin and John* vividly chronicles growing up gay in the South during the early decades of the twentieth century along with their close friendships with writers and artists of their era including Prentiss Taylor, Dorothy Heyward, Carson McCullers, Josephine Pinckney, and John Bennett. Most importantly, it lends insight into how a gay couple navigated the stages of first love, nesting, aging, and death. *Edwin and John* is a poignant portrait of two men in love.

As I have detailed in my other oral histories,[2] history is best understood through the narratives of everyday persons going about their daily lives against the panoply of larger social and political events. Although John gave me permission to write his story, it has been structured with him as narrator. This truly is "his story." I was pleased when John agreed to read and revise earlier chapters drafted from his published and unpublished writings, poetry, correspondence (including his and Edwin's remarkably extensive World War II letters), and our conversations—along with my interpretations of those.

Each of us is the author of our own life. I am not John, and I never met Edwin. I became friends with John in the early 1990s, long after Edwin had passed away, while researching Charleston's gay history.[3] In many ways, our generational experiences were quite different. I grew up as a homosexual Midwesterner in the 1950s. Unlike John, I learned, at a very early age, the penalty for being different—being queer. As part of the "Greatest Generation," Edwin and John freely entered the battlefield buoyed by patriotism in the face of fascism. Many of my generation took to the barricades resisting patriotic bromides, burning draft cards and flags, and marching on America's "war machine." Edwin and John's gay generation saw little value in coming out to friends, family members, or neighbors, viewing their gayness as simply another aspect of their personhood. My generation unleashed "gay liberation" to challenge the

Figure I.3 James Sears overlooks John Zeigler as they review his World War II correspondence.

hegemony of the closet. We built grassroots organizations, published magazines and wrote books, marched in pride down main streets before circling in silence to remember quilted names of our fallen comrades.

Bridging this generational divide was sometimes difficult. As we shuttled drafts back and forth, my understanding of John's worldview—one where *being* gay was never really an issue—deepened. He likely found annoying, at times, my requests for additional information about gay life and experiences. Sometimes John found it difficult to sleep at nights, as he sought to recollect a specific event, recall a face, or revise a paragraph. We both struggled to listen and accommodate the perspective of the other. And, in the end, this iterative process worked remarkably well, deepening our friendship.

Structuring this book in first-person narrative should engage the everyday reader but it may enrage a traditionally trained historian. But, as I have pointed out in my earlier book on the history of the Mattachine through the biographical story of Hal Call:

> In modernist scholarship, the interpretive hand is hidden behind passive verbs, third-person voice, detached narrative, and scholarly footnotes. Research, however, is subjective. . . . The critical test, I believe, is not objectivity but authenticity. Does the biography portray the complexity of the individual and the times? Does the

history enjoin the reader to bracket a worldview or suspend prior judgment? To what degree does the author empower readers to arrive at different (or even oppositional) conclusions or points of view? Does the reader engage in a recursive reading of his or her own life? In what ways does the book empower us to act upon the world as we now understand it?[4]

For interested readers, footnotes accompanying each chapter provide additional historical context, information relating to gay materials, or the specific source for a quote. But, a human being is not a footnote. People create history. Our story, as same-gender loving human beings, is ultimately about how each of us choose to live out our lives within a society which, at best, passes us by in silence, and, at worst, destroys us through word or deed. *Edwin and John* complicates understanding of our history, honors the human experience, and champions the human heart.

In Carson McCullers' first novel, *The Heart is a Lonely Hunter,* the homosexual deaf-mute aptly demonstrates the inability of others to show love or to soothe the loneliness of others. Edwin and John are the exception to McCullers' observation. "Most of us would rather love than be loved," she later wrote in her novella, *The Ballad of the Sad Café*. "Almost everyone wants to be the lover."[5] But, as Edwin and John show us, one can be both lover and beloved. Perhaps that is the secret to a half century journeying together.

Part I
Early Years

1   Clingman's Dome

> The moon was a great white smile in the autumn night,
> Its glow sifting down through the shadowy trees
> That lined the racing mountain stream. The boulders
> Summoned us for leaping and playing at childhood.
> Naked, we shouted, sang arias without beginning or end,
> Fell, finally, for the first time, into each other's arms
> As natural as moon, rocks, water, and knew that
> Together all was possible, that we had found an island
> In that marvelous evening of our birth
> From which no rescue was desired, or even possible
> A Memory, Fifty Years Later

I want to talk about the past—our past—but in doing so I know that what I say may not be completely true, for much has been forgotten. What seemed important at one time may seem less so now, and daily events are all scrambled up in the years that have passed, as it seems now, far too quickly. Some of the events related here are authenticated in my letters and photographs, but most of what I'm going to tell you is firmly placed in my memory—and gives me pleasure or pain now just as it did when it first happened.

It was a few days before the Fourth of July, 1940. I was working on a novel, putting aside my poetry for the time. I had returned after six years in Washington doing boring work at the Reconstruction Finance Corporation. But those dark Depression years in our nation's capital were lightened by warm friendships with a group of other gay men—some of whom you may already know—or think you know—from the diary of "Jeb," in the book, *Jeb and Dash*.[1] In Ina Russell's book, for the most part based on Carter's (he's Jeb) diary, I was recast as Little Nicky—and killed off by Ina in World War II. But more of that later.

Writing that afternoon in my aunt and uncle's rented summer cottage at the Isle of Palms, I heard a motorcycle. I went on the porch and looked down. A tall, slender figure in white shorts dismounted. He looked up and smiled.

4 *Early Years*

Figure 1.1 John (left) and Isham "Dash" Perkins circa 1950.

This must be Edwin Peacock, I thought. I had written him a few days before at the suggestion of our mutual friend, Topie Johnson, a cousin of Carson McCullers. She thought that we ought to get to know each other so I had invited him to dinner with my relatives to celebrate the Fourth.

When I looked into his chiseled face with honest eyes, a reflective brow, and a mass of dark, curly hair, I had the feeling that this was a person with whom a *real* friendship could be established. It was an instantaneous feeling, one I had never had before or after with another person.

Edwin had come to tell me that he had other plans for the holiday but could come on the Sunday following. It was a short visit, for he was working in the Finance Office at Fort Moultrie, an Army base, and was on his lunch break. The motorcycle had been borrowed and, he admitted later, was used to make an impressive introduction. Occasionally throughout our forty-nine years together he would delight in arriving at informal parties in outlandish attire; sometimes on roller skates or in jodhpurs with riding boots and a whip.

In no time, we had set up sort of a pattern of meetings. We were living about four miles apart. He usually walked over after supper from his boarding house. We would stroll on the wide beach talking of books and music, of our small-town pasts, my years in Washington and his at Fort Benning. He spoke often of his friends Carson and Reeves McCullers. When Carson sent him a copy of *The Heart is a Lonely Hunter,* just published, he loaned it to me after he read it.

As I came to know him, I knew that the character of Singer in the book had something of Edwin, who was slightly deaf, in him. As Carson wrote, "The other mute was tall. His eyes had a quick, intelligent expression. He was always immaculate and very soberly dressed . . . his face was eager and his gray green eyes sparkled brightly."[2] Too, the relationship between Singer and Mick (the young girl) resembled that between Edwin and Carson in her visits to him at his apartment in Columbus, Georgia.

Sometimes after a visit from Edwin, I walked part of the way back to his room or he might walk back part of the way with me so that we could continue our conversation. I began to write poetry again. I felt absolutely committed to this growing friendship and was ready for any eventuality. There was, though, a question in my mind as to just how strongly Edwin felt about me, or *even* if he was gay. In those days, you see, I was reticent, and homosexuality was not generally discussed. And, at thirty, Edwin had never had a strong relationship with anyone and seldom spoke of intimate feelings. He showed his feelings through deeds rather than words.

As the summer of 1940 raced to an end, I found myself back in Charleston at 9 College Street, the home of my great aunt Nina and my aunt Detie, both of whom loved me with an unselfish devotion. I gave Nina a pittance each month, wrote every day, and attended a playwriting group headed by Dorothy Heyward, widow of DuBose Heyward. Among us were Josephine Pinckney who was from the famous Pinckneys and wrote about Charleston's declining upper class; she would have been an even better writer if she had not been so discreet. Her first novel, *Three O'Clock Dinner,* was published in 1945 and became a bestseller. There was also a handsome tall woman with white hair, Laura Bragg. An émigré from New England, she had transformed the Charleston museum and championed such young artists and writers as William Halsey, Ned Jennings, and Richard Coleman.[3]

6 *Early Years*

I took that group extremely seriously and, within a year, wrote three not-so-very-good plays, one of which received a walk-through production at the Dock St. Theater's Green Room. *At Home with Miss Glover* was about 9 College Street and a family who had come from the mountains of Tennessee to work in the Navy Yard. Ginny, a young woman who played the violin badly, was a camp follower. Her boyfriend had been sent to Panama, and she didn't get along with the others. The couple lived with their two boys in the back of the house. And then there was the romantic interest of an English professor for the great aunt. I had written a song to go with the play—don't ask me to remember that.

Edwin came over frequently, sometimes having supper with us. He became a great favorite of my aunts and, indeed, had met Detie before he met me, as she, too, worked on Sullivan's Island and used the same boat that he took to and from Fort Moultrie. His time was always limited in the evenings as he had to catch the last boat. I began to feel frustrated because nothing had been settled between us as to the future; I could not imagine a time when we would *not* be seeing each other. It occurred to me that a hiking trip in the Blue Ridge and Great Smoky Mountains might bring us closer together. He liked the idea.

We started out, poorly equipped, in mid-September, taking a bus to Asheville, spending the night at the YMCA, and we began our hitchhiking the next day until we reached a spot where the trail could be easily taken.

The next two weeks were a good test of Edwin's commitment to me. I was not a good mountain hiker, getting out of breath when climbing and

Figure 1.2 Edwin at Smoky Mountains on trip to Clingman's Dome, 1940.

subject to an occasional nosebleed. However, I had determination and made every effort to keep up without complaining. There were marvelous compensations in the beauty of the forests, the rock streams, the ferns and occasional fall flowers, not to mention the grandeur of the views with the autumn foliage turning more and more the higher we climbed. And, then, of course, there was Edwin.

At Clingman's Dome there was an unearthly light coming through the great trees and I felt closer to some unseen power than I have ever felt since. Edwin reveled in everything, making notes of the flora, enjoying the physical activity. At night we often found a lean-to on the trail, sometimes sharing it with other hikers. At other times it was necessary to make a fire in a cleared spot. Our single blankets never kept out the cold as we approached October, but there was always something to talk about in those wakeful moments around the blaze. He learned my weaknesses. I felt safe in his strengths. Eventually, we reached Gatlinburg, then a small, rambling village, where we found a cabin beside a stream. It was along that stream that I was able to express my feelings for Edwin and to learn that these were reciprocated.

> Remembering mountains
> Where we clambered,
> Tumbling into gullies,
> Pulling at branches,
> Testing rocks in streams
> Where we bathed at dusk
> Before striving for sleep
> Beside twig fires or in
> Lean-tos come upon by chance;
> Leaping into the ferny morning
> Drunk on the still beauty
> Of ancient wilderness,
> Two spirits that wanted life
> To be a never-ending exploration,
> A soaring into the unexpected,
> A sharing that must be absolute,
> I know that we kept true
> To that first testing, that
> First run into a future
> Stretching endlessly.
>   Remembering

2   A Cure?

> Like a long-legged boy
> Riding the indifferent wave
> Before he spills
> I came to love
>   September Variations

I was born in Manning, South Carolina on February 5, 1912, four years before America's entry into World War I. My father was a druggist, and my mother had been a school teacher. Both were in their early twenties. By the time I was five and a half, we had lived in Marshall, North Carolina, Columbia and Lydia, South Carolina before moving to Florence. At that age, I entered the grammar school there and graduated from Florence High School in 1928—the year I entered The Citadel. There was no overriding reason for me to go to The Citadel: The choice was made by my mother because she had loved going to the Saturday-night dances at the military college. But, I am getting ahead of myself again.

I don't remember much about those first five years except for visits to my aunts and great aunts in Charleston, where I learned to read just before I was five in the private school run by my great aunts. The Great War meant nothing to me, but in the great flu epidemic of 1918 everyone in our family but my father was taken ill. Millions of people died of it worldwide.

In Florence, I led a rather sheltered life, though with responsibilities toward my two sisters and my brother, all of us born in a time span of less than six years. When my brother was born, I was not quite six and would walk blocks to buy groceries. When I was in eighth grade, I was trusted with my siblings when my parents went to the theater or elsewhere. I was even allowed to attend a traveling performance of the musical, *Smilin' Through,* which began my lifelong interest in theater.[1]

By then, my father had given up his profession as a pharmacist, which he got into because an uncle was Dean of the Pharmacy Department at the Medical University of South Carolina. He edited a weekly newspaper over the drugstore, and I would fold papers as they came off the press. When backers offered to make it a daily, it became *The Florence Morning News.* In 1925, he wrote *The Last of the Bighams,* based on his reporting of the mass-murder trial of Edmund Bigham. His editorials often criticized the Klan and Southern politicians whom he considered demagogues. One morning, when the white-robed men with hoods paraded by our home, we children hid under the house, pretending fear that the Klan would "get us" because of our father's fiery editorials and our mother's unrepentant Catholicism.

My parents were loving and not too strict. I realized later that, as the eldest, I had been experimented on a bit, with more following of rules than my younger siblings. Our two-story white-framed house was filled with music (the Edison in the living room was always playing opera) and books, a bone of contention between my parents as my father could never resist a book salesman and money was always a problem—even before the Depression. There were few children's books, except for the occasional Horatio Alger or Tom Swift. We read Thackeray, Twain, Dumas, and Dickens among others. The fourteen volumes of *The Secret Memoirs of the Courts of Europe* offered some titillation.[2] Although I was a good student, I was not a dedicated one. But, I was an avid reader. I'd always get some books for Christmas and would just sit and read. I was apt to bring a book to class, too, and read it surreptitiously, a habit that stayed with me through my Citadel years.

I liked my family and *some* of my cousins but made few attempts at friendship. I don't think I was effeminate, but I was fairly aloof—mostly from shyness which took me years to discard. There were, of course, a few friends. We made caves in the backyard where we spent the night. We jumped from trees into a great giving bush and staged plays in our garage.

I met my best friend, Edward Newbury, when we were about ten. He and I would often spend the night with each other. Cuddling led to more interesting activities, as we discovered that it was possible to give each other pleasure in simple and unsophisticated ways, which were to continue until we were sixteen. When he moved away, at thirteen, we exchanged holiday and weekend visits, which continued until I graduated from high school. My parents considered him one of the family, and we remained friends until his death at seventy-five.

Overriding all, however, was my great hunger for books. The beautiful, splendid librarian in Florence must have sensed this, urging me to read books beyond my years: all of Henry James, especially. Interestingly, her daughter would later marry the man who caught the bank robber John Dillinger in Chicago.

Sometimes I would leave the library and read by the winter moonlight as I walked to our new home at the edge of town. By the time I reached high school, I was reading the book review and arts section of the Sunday *New York Times* when it arrived by train every Monday or Tuesday.

This, of course, was the decade of the 1920s. So there were news stories like the Scopes Monkey Trial and the trial of Sacco and Vanzetti, Byrd flying over the North Pole, Lindbergh's flight to Paris, Amelia Earhart flying over the Atlantic, and the Stock Market crash. I have already mentioned the biggest local story about the Bigham murder and trials, but let me tell you a bit more. On January 15, 1921, Edmund killed his entire family: his mother, brother, sister and her two children. He always proclaimed his innocence, and there were a couple of trials which found him guilty. He cursed everyone who testified against him saying they would all die before he did—and four of them did! He told the court, "They've lied on me, and every one of them will die before I do." Following this, one witness had a heart attack, and, in all, four died before the end of his three trials![3]

I can't remember a time when I didn't have an interest in sex. In Edward's absence, I found several other willing boys of my age. These boyhood and teenage experiences were uncomplicated and unemotional, pleasant and tension-releasing. All of the other boys later married. I had no feelings of guilt. Should I have?

Years later when Edwin and I became lovers, he told me of his early childhood experiences in Thomasville. He was born in this southwest Georgia town on January 2, 1910, the seventh of eight children.

His father, too, was a druggist. Unlike me, there was very little sex of a shared nature in his early years. At twelve, he escaped the clutches of his scoutmaster. In his teens, Edwin fumbled around with his best friend in the church choir loft. (He was the pianist and had the keys to the church!)

There was another sexual experience as Edwin entered his twenties, with a farmer. Edwin moved to Columbus, Georgia, a Southern mill town with a nearby military base, to work at Fort Benning in the Civilian Conservation Corps. His front door was never locked. The milkman would enter and put the quart into the refrigerator. One day he passed the bathroom where Edwin, tumescent, was shaving. He told Edwin that he knew a farmer who could take care of "that." A meeting was arranged, and Edwin went out to the farmer's property and was taken into a cornfield, where oral sex was performed on him. As Edwin came out of the field, two young sons of the farmer taunted him: "Sissy! Sissy! Sissy!" They had observed the transaction. Edwin never returned to the farm. He had no further sexual contact with anyone until we met. He did, however, often visit on weekends the country place of two landscape gardeners who were older and had lived together for years.

It was in the spring of 1934 that Edwin met Carson Smith. She was still the gamin she would depict in her novels *The Member of the Wedding* and *The Heart is a Lonely Hunter*. She paid little attention to dress or appearance. Sometimes there was plainness in her face, but that would be transformed when she laughed at Edwin's stories of eccentrics he had

A Cure? 11

Figure 2.1 Edwin with sister Virginia at family Thomasville home, 1919.

known in Thomasville, especially Miss Essie, a hatmaker, better known for her malapropisms. She loved Radio City because of the beautiful statue of Promiscuous. Carson was a loner. Her hobby was reading, her passion playing the piano. She loved her piano teacher and found in Edwin her first adult friend.

Two years earlier, Carson had been misdiagnosed and left untreated for rheumatic fever, which caused her to abandon her hopes of becoming a concert pianist. This seventeen-year-old would become his most intimate friend until her death in 1967. They first met when they shared a ride with Carson's piano teacher, Mary Tucker, to attend a Rachmaninoff concert in Atlanta. Along the ninety-mile journey, Edwin and Carson picked flowers at Pine Mountain, joking and laughing as if they had known each other forever.

Soon afterward, Edwin moved into town and rented a small apartment. He bought a used spinet piano for 100 dollars, allowing Carson to play for him away from the Smith home, where he was a frequent and much admired visitor. Sometimes Carson was chided for "going out with that old man." But neither she nor Edwin, who was just twenty-four, paid any attention. They also pooled their phonographic records, forming a little group known as The Record Club.

To Carson, Edwin was the best-read person she had ever met. She shared with him a novel she had begun to write. He also typed some of her short stories for her and introduced Carson to the magazine *Story*, which would be the venue for her first publication "Wunderkind," in December 1936, about an insecure adolescent musical prodigy.

Edwin continued their friendship through correspondence when Carson sailed to New York City, in February 1935. She told him about working menial jobs and beginning night classes in creative writing at Columbia University. (One of her teachers would be Whit Burnett, who edited *Story* magazine.) Edwin wrote her about his friend, Corporal James Reeves McCullers. The two had met at the library, and Edwin had invited Reeves over to his house for drinks.

Reeves was a charming Southerner of Irish descent with gray-blue eyes who looked a few years younger than his twenty-two years. He had recently re-enlisted for another three years in the Army, where he worked as a clerk. Because of Prohibition, he and Edwin would sometimes cross the Chattahoochee River into Alabama for beer at a local brothel. Edwin was not interested in the girls.

Edwin also introduced Reeves to the Smith family, who quickly adopted him into their own. When Carson returned to Columbus that June, she first met Reeves at Edwin's apartment. Throughout that summer, while Carson reported for the *Columbus Ledger*, the three of them were constant companions. Sometimes, Reeves would borrow Edwin's bike to peddle the thirty miles to a Girl Scout camp where the two would swim, eat their boxed lunch, and play chess. Reeves was faithful to Carson. Within two years, Reeves and Carson were married.[4]

3 What Must One Do?

> Old man, I envy you—
> Your smile, and wrinkled face
> Speak much of peace.
> I wish that I were old,
> That all this aching youth was gone;
> That I could count my wrinkles
> And my memories, each, one for one.
> That all my vain self-pity
> Could be turned into the quiet
> Of the shaded brook, into the pebbles
> Made so smooth these many years
> As cares are smoothed away
> Old man, to be at peace with God,
> What must one do?
>   What Must One Do?

I entered The Citadel in the autumn of 1928. As I said earlier, it was not because of any fondness for military life but because of my mother's fond memories of the college's Saturday-night dances. I really should have gone to the College of Charleston, which was across the street from my aunts' house.

Day-to-day life at The Citadel was not as hard as it is today but many of the traditions that I experienced remain. As a "knob," one had to clean upperclassmen's rooms and run errands for them. I was unhappy at first, though I did not receive much hazing. It was also embarrassing as I was unused to sharing open toilets or showering collectively. I often waited until lights-out to perform such activities. I had nothing in common with my freshman roommate, a friend from high school. I did, however, enjoy the Saturday-night dances, and my interest in poetry developed in the first-year English class of the young James G. Harrison—the best teacher I ever had. I also enjoyed tennis, basketball, and swimming, but I skipped most of the football games when I could.

Years later, when Edwin and I were operating The Book Basement, we displayed in a window a new bestselling novel, *End as a Man*.[1] This was a story of two cadets who are out of place in an unnamed Southern military academy preparing officers during World War II. Caldwell Willingham, who was just twenty-four when he wrote the story, had attended The Citadel for a year. He described the sadism and bullying associated with the hazing ritual along with undertones of homoeroticism. At least one of the characters, Perrin, is portrayed as a homosexual who falls in love with the macho cadet Jocko. One afternoon, the charming librarian of The Citadel, who bought all of her books from us, saw the novel displayed and suggested that we remove it from the window before some official of the school saw it. She didn't want anything to jeopardize our relationship.

I didn't have a roommate when I began my second year at the military college, but there was a requirement that there should be two cadets in a room. I was reading Oscar Wilde's *Salome* when a junior whom I didn't know came in and talked a while. He left but later returned and asked if he could room with me. I said yes. It turned out we had many things in common, especially a love of classical music and good literature. We were soon reading the Russians, the French, and plays of Ibsen and Shakespeare, in which we took various roles.

We enjoyed walks together as well as our long conversations. We often strolled to town through Hampton Park, where I had been as a child to feed the ducks in the small pond. Sometimes we discussed freeing the birds from cages. We saved car fare by walking through some poorer neighborhoods where we saw the tree from which pirates were said to have been hanged. Then the large handsome houses would appear before we reached my great aunts, where we often had supper. Later we would walk to The Battery and enjoy the views from the seawall from which we could see the Ashley and Cooper rivers emptying into the Atlantic Ocean.

One evening, my friend decided that I should have a sexual experience with a woman. He bought condoms and took me to a little house where, for three dollars, I had a quick session with a middle-aged woman—as he watched. The experience didn't take.

Charleston was a sleepy city that had seen better days well before the Great Depression. I think the opening lines uttered by Porgy in DuBose Heyward's work, described it best "an ancient, beautiful city that time had forgotten before it destroyed."[2] During the Depression, rich and poor alike suffered in Charleston. Grand houses needed painting. The wellborn were taking in roomers and boarders, glad to have money, even if it was Yankee currency, coming in. The owner of perhaps the finest house in the city was one of those women who turned her ancestral home into a guest house. When one of her lodgers offered his copy of the Sunday *New York Times* to read, she refused to take it, saying that she didn't know anyone in New York.

What Must One Do? 15

Figure 3.1 John at Sullivan's Island, 1933.

In the summer, my friend and I took a holiday together to the coast north of Charleston. After a nude swim one night, we entered, for the first time, into a new relationship, which was to continue through the next school year as roommates.

I vividly remember one night walking together along a wharf. A seaman called down from the looming freighter and asked if we would like to come aboard. Once on board, we concocted a plan to stow away on it that night. Fortunately, we learned that the ship wouldn't sail for five days.

In my junior year, I went before The Citadel's Board of Visitors to request permission for a literary magazine to be published at the school. They agreed that it would be good for the school and arranged for it to be financed. A contest was held to find a name. The winning title was *The Shako*, representing the hat that is worn on dress occasions. At last I had a place to publish poetry, essays (one on Edna St. Vincent Millay) and stories, as well as the fine writing of my junior-year roommate. I was Editor my senior year also.[3] Captain Harrison was the faculty adviser.

At the end of the school year, just before graduation, my roommate had the day off and went to Folly Beach, where he swam far out into the Atlantic, wanting to drown. When he hadn't returned at a reasonable hour, I was filled with alarm. I learned later that he had changed his mind but then had trouble getting back to shore. He actually felt that he had, being two years older, seduced me.

When I was a senior, my time had become pleasant enough except for the sometimes overwhelming despair because of his departure. This was a relationship, however, which could not last as he was not truly a homosexual. In my last year at The Citadel, however, I had a delightful, intelligent roommate who was the editor of *The Bull Dog,* the college newspaper. He was several years older and had already fathered an illegitimate child with a local young woman. Sometimes he would slip out over a fence to meet her.

In the fall of my senior year, a senior military officer, who also wrote poetry, invited me to accompany him to a meeting of the Poetry Society of South Carolina's writing group. There I got to know experienced writers such as Katherine Simons, Josephine Pinckney, and John Bennett. The Society was uniquely Charleston. It had been founded twelve years earlier as the first local group in the U.S.A. to promote the appreciation of poetry. Writing members shared their work in the writers' group anonymously with others, allowing a newcomer like myself to be read along with Pinckney and others. The Society hosted guests who would give a reading before the membership. Such writers as Amy Lowell, Gertrude Stein, and Edna St. Vincent Millay would read their poetry. An older woman friend told me years later that she took Millay and her husband to see one of the beautiful Charleston gardens. She said it was the only time in her life when she was propositioned by both a husband and wife on the same day.

The era known as the "Charleston Renaissance," began with the founding of the Poetry Society and included artists as well as writers. There were Alfred Hutty, Elizabeth O'Neill Verner, and Alice Ravenel Huger Smith and others. There was also a thriving group at the Dock Street Theater and the vibrant Charleston Museum under the forward looking leadership of Laura Bragg.[4]

We were asked in the writers' group to create an ode to be read at the Confederate Memorial Day exercises at Magnolia Cemetery. Mine happened to be chosen. This was my first sort of "recognition," but I was too shy to read the poem on the platform before the crowd and my fellow cadets. It was read by an Englishman, a member of the Poetry Society. Although he made two errors in the reading, covering me with embarrassment, his delivery was first-rate.

When I graduated in June of 1932, I returned home to Gastonia, North Carolina, where my family had been living for three years. In the depth of the Great Depression there were no jobs. With a college graduate neighbor, whose roommate had been Carson McCullers' cousin, Topie Johnson, we set up a classroom in my home to continue the education of my two sisters, unable to attend college because of lack of funds.

One day, just before Christmas, I received a letter from my former roommate and lover urging me to come to Washington and establish a life together. Around New Year's Day, I got a ride to our nation's capital. I arrived in freezing weather only to find when I got to his rooming house that he had been called back to North Carolina because of the illness of a sister. I stayed on for a few days, ate a lot of peanut butter and bread, and roamed the cold streets where the homeless were warming benches or huddling in doorways.

I returned to Florence to stay with my grandmother Zeigler and was offered the editorship of a new weekly newspaper; my sister, Virginia, became the paper's business manager. The problem was that we were never paid! After a couple of months she got a job at the Department of the Interior through the office of Jimmy Byrnes, as my father called his South Carolina friend. I went to Charleston and procured a job with the WPA (Works Progress Administration) at Bennett Elementary School, teaching mathematics and English to children with learning disabilities in groups of five. Many of the students were from a nearby orphanage. My only embarrassment there was the morning when I was asked to referee a baseball game in the absence of the coach. It was obvious to the kids that I didn't know much about that sport.

As summer approached, I was eager to move on. When a job was found for me at the Reconstruction Finance Corporation in Washington, I moved. During the six years there, I would meet some remarkable people. I was more or less a twenty-two-year-old innocent who had never heard the word "homosexual" or given a name to my feelings, which seemed quite natural.

During my first couple of years at The Citadel, Edwin was working at his father's drugstore in Thomasville. There was no money for college. His father was from the fairly nearby town of Pavo. Years earlier, when the residents got together to incorporate it, they couldn't agree on a name, each wanting to name it for his family. A Peacock offered a compromise. "Why not name it Pavo?" The others agreed, not knowing that Pavo is Latin for Peacock. There seem to be advantages in being smarter than your neighbors.

Edwin's mother was brought up in a handsome plantation home, Greenwood, surrounded by 3,000 acres of mostly woodland. Her mother was left with the management of the plantation after the men of the family were killed in the War Between the States. By the end of the nineteenth century, she could no longer cope with the responsibilities and sold it. Eventually it came under the ownership of the well-known Whitney family, who would one day give it to the State of Georgia. Mother and daughter moved into a bungalow in Thomasville, which the mother bought when her daughter married. She lived in a small house in the back garden while her daughter, Marion, produced eight children, of which Edwin was the seventh.

This was a happy family, full of wit, curiosity, and a willingness always to share. Fifteen-year-old Martha played the piano in the movie theater. Another sister picked up her neighbor's pecan crop, shared them, and made goodies to sell in the drugstore. The older sister dressed up one day as a mature woman and, wearing a hat and veil, took two of the younger girls with her to inquire if there was a room she and her children could rent at a rooming house. She asked if she was nearing the tropics and if there was a subway in town. When the proprietor came upstairs with a pitcher of ice water, she suddenly recognized Sarah and said, "Sarah Peacock you always were crazy!" The Peacock family often played jokes on neighbors or each other, but they were always harmless.

Thomasville was a beautiful town to which rich Northerners came to winter. Edwin was always attracted to interesting older people, those of the town and those who brought a taste of the outside world. One of his most respected friends was the Rector of the Episcopal Church, whose wife expected to see him barefoot at the pulpit one day because he gave so many of his clothes to the needy. One time the minister was asked if he wasn't particularly blessed. He replied, "Yes, when you consider the fact that I have a son who writes immoral novels, a daughter who has a habit of marrying rich men, and a wife who is perfectly agreeable as long as she is having her own way."

Edwin's botany hobby led him to take freight trains into the woods, jumping off and returning home, gathering wild flowers or mushrooms. There was a splendid botanist in town (she corresponded with Laura Bragg) who loved sharing her knowledge with Edwin. He was perhaps the last person to see her conscious when he brought a mushroom to her sick bed. Almost in a coma, she smelled it and gave him its Latin name. She never spoke again.

He knew of the casual relationship between his best friend, Frank, with whom he had carried on in the church loft, and the older Minor, who often played bridge with one of Edwin's older sisters. One night Edwin accompanied a friend to the home of this friend's acquaintance who wanted to show them a pornographic film, which would be Edwin's first. After they arrived, the man's wife left for her duties as a night nurse. They were served beer, and the film began. Shortly afterward, the man offered them his pre-teen daughter and son for sex. Revolted, Edwin and his friend immediately left. Years later, Edwin and I would see our first pornographic film at a small theater in Havana, where in the hedonistic atmosphere of Batista's Cuba, it seemed almost natural.

Edwin was happy to seek wider horizons when he was accepted into the Civilian Conservation Corps and went to work at Fort Benning in a civilian capacity.

4   The Incident

> Lie with your arms around my breast
> Sleep your sweet gentle sleep. . . .
>
> > To You, Sleeping

Edwin and I continued down to Highlands from Clingman's Dome. There, having covered almost 200 miles, we were loaned a cottage by a Thomasville friend of Edwin—one of the many Miss So-and-Sos of whom he often talked. We spent a night at Lake Lure before going to Charlotte for a couple of days to visit my old childhood friend, Edward Newbury and his companion, Bob Walden, with whom he would live for over forty years.

Returning to Charleston, we faced, at least from my point of view, problems in our newly formed relationship. It was natural that we should be separated during the day, but I felt that the evenings should be "ours" —together and alone. He would come into town after work, and we would go to a movie, walk, or sit in my attic room talking of books or listening to records. Sometimes we could be intimate but it never seemed just right for him to spend the night with my aunts nearby. We both wanted more possibilities in the relationship.

After Christmas we decided that we would hitchhike to Key West for a few days. That was a time when hitchhiking was common and safe. The first ride, however, was a disaster. We were picked up by a drunk who drove at ninety miles an hour. We made excuses to get out and took the first bus that came along!

Key West was wonderful. It was inexpensive even on my income, which limited me to fifty dollars a month. Edwin's salary was probably not much more than twice that. This was a lazy holiday, lolling on the beach every day, spotting cheap restaurants or sometimes buying provisions to make our own cold meals. We met a gay couple who ran a candy store and joined them for beers a couple of times, but we weren't looking for others.[1] All we wanted was to be together. Occasionally, we spoke pidgin English with Spanish-speaking families on the beach. After a week, we were short of funds. Being the more practical one, I saw that there was enough left to get us back to Charleston. Reluctantly, we packed our bathing suits and headed home.

Between the New Year and early spring, Edwin continued to work for the War Department at Fort Moultrie, which is just across the river from Charleston on Sullivan's Island. I typed away at my novel. By the spring of 1941 we had become subject to the draft. I hated the thought of being drafted in South Carolina and being sent to Fort Jackson, on the outskirts of Columbia, known for its intense summer heat and humidity. I suggested to Edwin that we go out to Santa Fe and get drafted there, where we would be in a new environment. Edwin's Thomasville friend, Minor, had often urged him to come out for a visit to the spectacular mountains and desert.

Edwin resigned his job, and, at the end of April, we set out by bus for New Mexico by way of Thomasville and New Orleans. Along with my clothes, I hauled some books, including Mann's *The Magic Mountain* and several volumes of Proust. Mann was my favorite because of his human quality and, perhaps, also because of the homoerotic undertones in much of his work. Typical of Edwin, he was happy with my choices, having been a serious reader all of his life. He did bring a book on botany, which was a lifelong interest.

After the all-night bus ride from New Orleans, where we had little time to sample the gay bars that have been so much a part of its history, we were warmly greeted upon our arrival at Minor's homestead.[2] He was a somewhat older gay friend, independently wealthy after the death of his parents. He knew many parts of the world, having taken groups on guided tours in his earlier years. We stayed a couple of days at his isolated, handsome ranch home situated on 100 acres of desert.

We found a small house near the village of Tesuque, just five miles from Santa Fe. This was our first home. Our boxy white house stood on a little incline above a large *arroyo*, in which we never saw any water. The land came down from the highest ridge in waves, and we could imagine water coursing down it and sweeping through the house. There was a glassed-in sun room with a bed and another all-purpose room with a sink at the rear. A little stoop outside at the back had a showerhead in the rough ceiling and, some 60 yards further, hidden by some pinion trees, was the privy. We always worried if we would find a rattler there! The landscape behind the house, reddish like brick dust, was rather bare except for scrubby yellowish junipers, the occasional yellow rabbit brush, and the pinions.

From the front of our house, the road to the left led to Tesuque, a village with a beer parlor and a small general store. Nearby was the Tesuque Indian Mission. Some evenings we would walk the quarter of a mile or so to the village for a beer or two at the very unexciting El Nido's, rarely speaking to anyone. We could afford such "luxuries" as I could live

Figure 4.1 John at home out of Santa Fe, New Mexico, 1941.

nobly here on fifty dollars a month; we paid just twenty for rent. Aside from a potter and his wife who lived on our side of the *arroyo*, none of the people scattered in the hills were within yelling distance.

When we took the road to the right, we were on our way to Santa Fe. We hitchhiked there for groceries. Sometimes we were given rides by one or both of the great Russian duo-piano team of Vitya Vronsky and Victor Babin, when they weren't on a world tour or being mentored by their friend, Sergei Rachmaninoff. Often during the day we heard them practicing over the hill that rose between us. We'd stop what we were doing just to listen.

Years later, we were invited to meet them in Charleston when they were given a party by Josephine Pinckney after a concert. But during that New Mexican summer we were starved for music to which we now had no access as Santa Fe wasn't the cultural mecca it is now. There was a fine bookstore and *one* art gallery. The yellow, nineteenth-century Romanesque cathedral of Archbishop Lamy seemed then, as it does now, to rise out of the hills behind it, bringing into physical reality Willa Cather's great novel, *Death Comes for the Archbishop*, where she fictionalized him as Father Jean Latour and painted with words the primal beauty and history of the Southwest.

This was a fascinating town for us to explore. The bright gardens, usually enclosed, set in sharp contrast to the white of the adobe buildings. Here we eventually got to know a few people casually, some of them friends of Minor, who was not in a relationship at the time. His lesbian friends, Scoop and Julie, had had good jobs in California, but wanted the adventure of raising goats on a small parcel of land out of the city. They rolled their own cigarettes. Once they sent some of the tobacco with goat pellets to the manufacturer who promptly shipped them a winter's supply of tobacco with apologies.

We settled into our new life with the ease of novelty, conscious that this would be a time of testing further our relationship. At twenty-nine, I was rather set in my ways, still timid in some respects. Edwin was bold, adventurous, always willing to take chances, eager for the unknown. Intellectually, however, we met on equal terms, and there would never be a time during the next nearly fifty years together when we disagreed on the perplexing moral issues that would mark each of the five unfolding decades.

Our first few days, though, were spent exploring the countryside. At first, this meant long walks in either direction on the bed of the *arroyo*, where we learned to distinguish fireweed and butterfly weed, Indian paint brush (or "painted cup" as Edwin, the botanist, called them), penstamen (a kind of wild snapdragon), yellow daisies, primrose, lupin, yucca, low growing verbena, and, along the banks, an occasional cottonwood or yellowwood, as it was sometimes called. There were tamarisks about, too, with their sprays of lilac colored bloom, and bright acacias. When we began to build a rock garden, just behind the house, we had an enormous nursery before us from which we could choose, with many more plants whose names we didn't yet know. Fortunately, we never lacked for water and could pamper our garden as well as ourselves with frequent showers. Also, we never lacked for love as we pampered each other.

Before you conclude that I am being too misty-eyed at this point in my life, during that summer there occurred an incident, the cause of which I do not even remember. But, for some reason, I felt, one morning, that I'd been grievously wounded by Edwin. We were to go over to the potter's for drinks and supper in the evening. When Edwin took off for a short hike, after lunch, I made up my mind—angry and hurt—to go into Santa Fe and let my feelings simmer down.

I went to the bookstore, the art gallery, and generally ambled around town until dark. I wanted him to worry, as I often did when he was hiking in the mountains; for a few hours I didn't much care what happened to me. Eventually, I began the five-mile trek to Tesuque. I have never been more scared. I was walking on a dark two-lane highway with hills to my right and a steep slope to my left. I tried to outguess advancing cars or those coming from behind. When I returned, I was exhausted but indeed pleased to find that Edwin had been greatly worried about me. He had gone to the dinner and made excuses for me, and, when he returned only to find me still missing from home, wondered if he should get the police to begin a search. The very next day we were good friends again as we discussed the night's incident without rancor.

This taught us something that we needed to learn at that early point in our relationship: We were part of a team, and our responsibilities were to each other and us as a couple, not simply to ourselves as individuals. This has nothing to do with giving up individualities, which we kept until the end, but has everything to do with enabling the fulfillment of each individual through another human being who is loved, respected, and—yes—occasionally pampered.

Besides enjoying our developing relationship, we also pursued individual interests—an important strategy for any couple who wishes to remain together. I settled down to continue work on my novel, which I had begun when living in a Washington, D.C. apartment building along with Carter and Perks, whom many of you now know as "Jeb and Dash." During the day, Edwin would go off across the *arroyo*, over the red hills at the foot of the Sangre de Cristo Mountains and onto the mountain itself. The summer of 1941 was a dry one, but the sky was almost always filled with extraordinarily beautiful clouds hanging in a clear blue sky. The landscape changed with the clouds' shapes or sizes. I never got tired of looking up from my typewriter to observe this interplay between Heaven and Earth. We longed, though, for a Wagnerian thunderstorm that would bring the *arroyo* to watery life.

Usually I would stop writing by mid-afternoon, and then there would sometimes be anxious moments as I awaited Edwin's return as evening approached. Following "the incident," however, these moments of anxiety were fewer and less intense—although I never ceased to be just a bit worried.

On June 14, I received my first letter ever from George Scheirer, whom I had known slightly in Washington but who would become our closest friend and confidant during the coming war years. He began his letter, awkwardly acknowledging our loose friendship, "Perhaps you will wonder who I am."[3] But I didn't think that was deserved as I had never forgotten him. George was Managing Editor of the *Army Medical Bulletin* but he was, in his spare time, a pianist and an expert bookbinder. He was in his late thirties, very short, with a humpback—the result of a childhood illness. You ceased to notice these physical traits because of his wonderfully expressive face. He loved beauty in all of its forms and bore his disability with great grace.

I think the most embarrassing experience in my life occurred one afternoon when we happened to meet at Dupont Circle in Washington and sat on a bench to talk. Even then this was an area where gay men congregated. A member of Jehovah's Witnesses came up to us and urged us to buy a pamphlet. We politely refused, which brought on a tirade from the man, citing George's deformity as a blow from God because of his godlessness. This would-be avenging angel wouldn't go away so we left our bench and walked in silence for a few minutes.

I wrote George the day I received his letter: "it's flattering for someone to want news of me."[4] I had always enjoyed being with him, although I only saw him a few times during my six years in Washington. As a twenty-two-year-old and new to the "big city," I was in awe of George's intelligence and his accomplishments. It was only through an artist friend, Joe, who lived in my first rooming house, that George and I would meet. "I often wondered," I wrote, "after I had stopped seeing you just why I had. I believe it was shyness . . . " In a later letter, I told George:

> You know, it really isn't very wild out here. Wide open spaces, yes, but among the people of Santa Fe there is that same artificiality which you speak of as being in centers of population. It may have been tamed down a bit out here, but I am reminded of it, especially on Sunday afternoons when a few second-rate painters gather next door to paint the mountains. One of them has a beard, one has a library consisting of about twenty-five books on abnormal psychology. . . . There are a whole crop of Buddhist philosophers, hundreds of painters, and no end of writers . . . La Farge, Witter Bynner, Lynn Riggs, but they stay hidden for the most part down in their valleys. . . . I think that both of us have offended possible friends out here by turning down invitations.[5]

Turning down invitations allowed us more time together and for me to stay focused on my writing. I explained to George that during my last couple of years in Washington I was saving up my money to be able to write "for a couple of years," returning to Charleston in 1940. "I have written about 35,000 words," I told George. "It had rather a tough beginning as I have been pretty upset about the draft for the last few months." Now, in my defense, I had not even been able to rent a typewriter until the very week George's letter arrived—and I was pleased to write to him on this handsome machine that "the novel . . . seems to be going much better."

Another highlight of those months was the visit of Topie Johnson, who had introduced Edwin to me the year before. She was on her way to Hawaii to be an exchange teacher. When Pearl Harbor was bombed later that year, she was forced to return to the States. I listened with delight to stories of Carson, her family, and various odd characters who had come into their lives.

5   Lean Wolf Hours

In the summer of 1933, I returned to Washington and began working for the Reconstruction Finance Corporation. I mainly typed minutes of what seemed to be an endless array of agency meetings. Everything had to be done without erasures as they were going into permanent files. My office was a friendly place, and I liked all of the women with whom I worked— I was the only male typist. One of them became a lifelong friend who was to become the best friend of my nephew and his wife when they later came to live in Washington.

At first I was working from four until midnight. I went to George Washington University in the mornings and studied library science until my working hours changed to normal daytime ones. I never went back to the university but while there I had met and become friends with Dee Brown and his wife. He would later become well known as the author of the fine *Bury My Heart at Wounded Knee*.

During that first year in our nation's capital, I lived with my sister and did not meet anyone to share my sexuality. I first stayed at her rooming house from which we soon moved to a small apartment. At the rooming house, I met the artist, Joe Tucker, who also lived there. His wife had not yet joined him, and we often walked in the parks, talking about literature and the like.

One evening Joe invited me to go with him to visit his friend, George Scheirer. When we arrived at his apartment, George greeted us warmly, and, before long, I felt as though I had known him for months instead of minutes. He had a baby grand piano and, at our urging, played for us. Most of his friends were musicians or artists, and he often won first prize in the Miniature Society for his exquisite bindings of miniature books. I listened raptly to their stories of friends and their achievements or about books, plays, or musical events they had experienced since last meeting. I was intimidated because they knew so much more than I did.

There was no talk of sexuality, which was perfectly normal then when friends got together. But it was clear to me that George had no interest in girls. It was never a question of labeling anything. There were no labels attached to anything. I don't think most of us said, "We are homosexual." Looking back at it now, though, it is clear to me that George became, as our correspondence grew, in love with me.

One of my great pleasures then and during my years in Washington was going to a fine second-hand bookstore near my office during the lunch hour. I wasn't aware of gay novels such as *A Scarlet Pansy* or *Strange Brother*, but I had read *The Well of Loneliness*.[1] I was a rather discriminate buyer, with Ellen Glasgow, James Branch Cabell, Theodore Dreiser, and Sherwood Anderson among my favorite American writers.

On my way back from a Work Progress Administration (WPA) writing class in the evening, I would often walk up to Dupont Circle.[2] I'd stand there just watching the cars, waiting for the light to turn green. On a late October evening, my sister would have just gone for her weekly piano lesson. There was the first fall coolness in the air and in the things one saw. The trees almost bare of leaves, the men in sweaters or topcoats, the women in coats or jackets, the students hurrying to small rooms intent on the future. The moon was more distant, the mind sharper to the season's promises, the ears attuned to the new pitch of autumn sounds, the body aware of the wind's insistence. It was a time of year when one put aside the dreaming, the ambling of the mind through its lazy byways. The unplanning days were over.

For me, so many decades ago, standing on the street corner, waiting for that light to change, my season was still unplanned, except that the day hours were for work and the early night hours for the writing class. It was the lean wolf hours after the day was over that were free and, being free, empty for me. And that was why I was waiting now to cross the street and find a vacant bench in the park.

If I had found that bench on that autumn evening, I would have sat there until I grew tired of shifting positions and discovering leaf patterns in the light and wondering about the people who were alone and slow walking. I might have sat there an hour, or two hours, or just ten minutes before feeling an energy, a deep need for movement, a stinging loneliness that sent me walking again. Down to the bridge, to the dark roads in the park where there were bridle paths to follow and get lost in. To the noisy streets, where there were theater crowds to mingle with, to hurry through, to give a glancing blow to one's thoughts before they grew too arrogantly self-pitying.

Living in Washington as a gay man in my early twenties, there were places of darkness and the light places. I liked best the dark, where I could rid myself of the need of people. The parks I liked because they were dark and yet there was the lightness of people passing through them; so that when I had the feeling of needing companionship the parks gave more of it than the gaudy streets. Yes, I liked the dark, in parks, on a river, walking down a road, in a Rembrandt painting, in some of Tchaikovsky's music. Wherever it might be, before I met Edwin, I liked the dark.

I grew tired of waiting for the light to change. My feet shifted as I looked for something to lean against, and then I decided to return home.

I turned and walked back along Connecticut Avenue, peering into all the shop windows. Seeing for the hundredth time a small Chinese prayer rug offered at a "GREAT REDUCTION," looking at the expensive sophistication of Durand's shop, cork and aluminum hors d'oeuvres trays, glass bookends, and then somewhere a slow-moving cockroach unconcernedly trespassed over these objects.

I watched the people whom I passed, imagining that they did not know that I was watching them. I'd look at a face and see it as a face bare of emotion and I would insert some emotion on it. The people I saw, at that moment, were what I made of them. The cut of a woman's coat, the angle of a man's hat, the blowing of hair from behind the ears, all of these made an image on a face for me that was more real than any actual expression a face might possess.

If I thought someone gave me more than a passing glance, I'd look away quickly, to a light blinking, to a car stopping, to anything obvious. I would have liked for someone to speak to me, but I would have been embarrassed, a little afraid if they had. I had been in this town for six months but had not really met people outside of work.

Within a block of G Street, I began to walk more slowly. I lived just a block down G, off Connecticut. There was a weight all over me as I thought of returning to my apartment. It was like thunder pressing on my ears and water filling my nostrils. I wanted to throw bricks through windows, to scream out and stop the world, to run if it would have meant running anywhere. To do anything that would call attention to myself, that would hold me in light, noise, and movement.

I was examining pottery in a display window when I glanced to the left and saw a man, slightly older than I, look at me with an expression that drew us into a ring. Suddenly, I was cold all over and wondered if I was visibly trembling as I felt that the man was going to speak. I didn't want to leave the situation. It was as if I had broken a window and had been caught and held to answer for it. I was elated but my emotion held me tightly.

When the man spoke, at first in generalities, he seemed to be sizing me up. I had to laugh, although I didn't know why, unless it was to keep me from trembling so. Maybe I couldn't help laughing, knowing that I wouldn't be alone for a while.

He moved closer to me. Our elbows touched. I saw him looking at me as I wondered whether it was my turn to make the next move. I couldn't think of anything to say or do. Suddenly I wanted him to go away yet at the same time was afraid he would.

Soon he became quite frank and asked if I was interested in having sex with him. I quickly answered yes. He asked if I had a place to which we could go. I suggested my apartment.

We turned and went along the next block in silence.

28 *Early Years*

I looked at him from time to time and smiled with some deliberateness. There was lightness in his voice.

As soon as we entered, I pulled the Murphy bed down, and he started undressing, so I did, too. In bed, I closed my eyes and felt the soft warm lips touching my penis. Before I knew it, he was giving me my first oral sex. As Nietzsche said, "How shall man force nature to yield up her secrets but by 'unnatural acts'?"

When he finished, he jumped out of bed, put on his clothes, and left with a "thank you." I tidied the bed and put it back into the wall. When my sister returned, I was reading.

A few days later, I decided to linger in front of the window again. That evening, I met Phil Bell, an artist who taught in the WPA program and had done murals for department stores. He was a few years older, attractive, and easy to be with. We became friends after that first night in his studio.

Before long, he was introducing me to others in his circle, which included Carter and Perks (Jeb and Dash in the edited diaries where he was Max).³ I met his old friend Perks, who rented him a bedroom in his third-floor apartment. Later, I met Carter in that apartment. I was no longer a lonely gay man in the big city.

In the summer of 1935, my sister married, and I moved into a house where I had a large room with a nook to hold a refrigerator. I now had a place where I could bring my friends—gay or straight. Sometimes I taught bridge to some of my women friends.

From time to time I would walk over to Meridian Hill Park on Sixteenth Street around ten in the evening. If no one was about, I would

Figure 5.1 (From left to right) Phil Bell "Max," Carter "Jeb," and John "Little Nicky".

lean on the parapet, from which I could look down and see water streaming toward the front of the park. I would sing arias, tenor, baritone, or soprano, as loud as I could. I had heard opera since I was a small child and had sung in a Catholic Church choir throughout my teens. Although my voice was untrained, I needed to make sounds in the silence.

In the spring of 1936, the apartment beneath that of Perks and Phil became vacant. Perks suggested that Carter and I rent it since their guests would have to pass through the lower floor in order to get to their place. To enter the apartments you first had to walk through an entrance that led to an Italian restaurant, located on the ground floor. Upstairs would be our place. The stairway divided part of the apartment from the other. Carter would have the two large front rooms overlooking the street, and I would have the back room and kitchen. We would share a bathroom but would be entirely separate otherwise. My move was very simple, Carter's more difficult as he was not very good at practical matters. We helped him pack after we painted his rooms. He was eager to move and be closer to Perks.

By that time, I had met Bo, when we shared a ride into the country with a mutual friend. He came home with me that night and remained my lover until I left Washington. He was a few years older and lived with his family. He was a true craftsman and could make over furniture that was falling to pieces so that it looked new. He built Carter's bookshelves and a bookcase for me. We differed in many ways, I being much more liberal. I loved him but was not "in love." He came to my apartment several nights a week. I would prepare dinner, and if we had extra money we would go to the theater or a movie. I often felt annoyed about the little time I had for writing. A pastime that was mutually enjoyable was rowing on the Potomac some Sundays. He had much knowledge of Chinese art and ceramics, and, many years later, he and Edwin went to China together when I felt that the food there would not agree with my delicate stomach. While we were together, I never lingered before a store window. Dionysus and Apollo, reason and emotion, met equally in me for the first time.

Although Carter, Perks, Phil, and I were four gay men living in close proximity, we did not live a very "gay" lifestyle. There was no campiness in our interactions. All of us except Carter had good women friends. Nell, who is Pamela in the edited diaries, was a somewhat older French teacher. We would go to her handsome home for family functions with her sisters, who taught Latin and English. Occasionally, in the summer, there was watermelon in the backyard or swimming parties at her country club. Perks also had women friends from his photography club and hiking group, The Wanderbirds. Sometimes there would be gatherings to show photographs. His charm, wit, and unselfishness were the glue that held us together.

Carter was a loner. He was sensitive, and his feelings were easily hurt. He was always seeking in another the Perks he had fallen in love with years before in a romance that had only lasted a few months. They had remained good friends, but Carter *always* loved Perks. On many a night, Carter would wander out and drink until he had mustered the courage to sit on a park bench hoping to find someone he could bring back to the apartment if not into his life. This sometimes led to unpleasant results—a robbery, a demand for money.

Sometimes I would knock on his door in the morning, urging him to get up and go to work. He would answer that he was calling in sick despite his responsible position as an editor in a government office.

No one else in the apartment house really drank. Except for Carter, we were an easygoing group, each with his own interests. If doors were left open on our floor (and they often were during Washington's steamy summers), someone might stop for a moment to say hello or suggest going to Allies Inn for dinner. Straight friends came for visits but never seemed aware we were gay. People rarely stopped at Carter's apartment, but, if his door was open, as it often was, Carter would join them if they went to Perks.

We always had something to talk about, which was rarely gossip. We read, went to the theatre or the symphony. Carter read many of the books I did, and we often exchanged them. Because of his deep-rooted Southernness, I was surprised to see a number of books about Lincoln in his library. He told me once that they were all about the assassination.

We were more like a dormitory of gay men than a little gay social clique. On special occasions, such as New Year's Eve or a birthday, there would be a party in Perks' apartment or at Phil's studio. Nell would always be there, as would Jack, my writing friend, who was straight. No one seemed to think anything of two of us men dancing, while Nell danced with one of us.

One of the most pleasant things Perks, Jack, Bo, and I would do was to take the train to Harper's Ferry for a weekend of camping along the river with hikes into the surrounding hills. Once we were driven to Rehoboth Beach, where I was distressed at an entrance sign that said "No Jews Allowed." I wanted to turn around but had to accede to the wishes of the others for a swim. It was about that time that I heard Thomas Mann lecture on the situation in Spain and the persecution of Jews in Germany.

With Jack and two women, Jane and June, from the WPA writing class, we began publishing a "little magazine" out of my apartment. The four of us spent a lot of time together bringing out this quarterly. The year after I departed, Washington *Foothills* was stopped when Jane committed suicide because of recurring health problems. The four of us wrote and worked easily together, listened to my records, and were happy in our friendship. The magazine was mimeographed, and our group published early stories of the Quaker writer, Jessamyn West, whose 1945 book, *The Friendly Persuasion*, was a critical success.

In early 1940, I decided that I must have time to write the novel I had in mind. I hated to hurt Bo, who didn't want me to leave, but I was determined. I had managed to save 1,000 dollars and felt that I could live on fifty dollars a month, staying with my great aunt in Charleston. There was a very pleasant farewell party for me following a dinner with Bo's mother and sister, both of whom I admired. I felt that his mother understood the relationship between Bo and me for she thanked me for having been a special friend to him.

Almost all of the gay friends I knew in Washington worked for government agencies without any problem about their homosexuality. That was to change, of course, during the McCarthy years when Perks and another friend had to leave their jobs of decades at the State Department, along with many others. Another friend, a librarian at the Weather Bureau, was told to resign. The next day, he returned to his office, sat at his desk, and shot himself in the head.

> St. Matthew and the elm trees cast
> Their shadows down as in the past,
> But Jack and June and John and Jane
> Shall never pass this way again.
> Longfellow, rusting on the square,
> The Old Italian on the stair,
> No longer listen for a tune
> From Jack and John and Jane and June,
> For river-flowing time destroys
> The deepest dreams of girls and boys
> And makes four islands where was one
> Land of poetry and sun
> And Jane, who lies beneath the ground,
> And John, who sails the earth around,
> And Jack, who cuts away the sky,
> And June, who teaches men to fly,
> Shall meet no longer in the lake
> Of shade the church and elm trees make.
>   Washington Story

Part II
War Years

6   A Yeoman's Journey

Around summer's end in 1941, Edwin and I found that our money was running out. In the middle of August, we had house guests. Jack Deasy, a member of the literary group in Washington that put out *Foothills* magazine, arrived in New Mexico in a beat-up old car which somehow got us to Taos and other places of interest. He was a tall, finely featured fellow with a passion for the outdoors and for writing. At that time, I thought he was the most talented writer among my friends, perhaps destined for the highest reaches of literature.

My Aunt Detie, a wiry creature of the most generous, natural sensibility, also visited. I can give no better description of her than to say that she resembled in looks the great French writer Colette. She adored me, loved Edwin, and found New Mexico the most wonderful place she had ever visited. Though she had always lived a relatively comfortable life at 9 College Street, she adapted easily to our rather primitive way of life. She and I would talk of family, of her own romantic, if sad, past, or we would read, take a walk in the *arroyo*, plan a method for her to take a bath while Edwin and Jack went out exploring the mountain. Edwin was also writing to several army finance offices around the West, giving his qualifications, telling of his experiences in the finance offices at Fort Benning and Fort Moultrie.

After Jack left, while Detie was still with us, a telegram came from the Finance Officer in San Francisco. He had been Edwin's boss at Fort Moultrie, and he asked that Edwin come out at once.

On September 1, we packed our odd belongings, pots, pans, sheets, food, and were driven into Santa Fe by Minor, whom we had seen rarely during the summer. Joining us on our bus ride to San Francisco was Detie, who had another week of holiday and was delighted to be going further west. Since the trip took us through Los Angeles, we stopped to see Edwin's sister, Mignon, whose boyfriend had us for drinks in his apartment and took us on a tour of the drapery department at the Fox movie studio where he worked. Those few hours in Hollywood were like a crazy dream: "This is the restaurant where Thelma Todd was last seen alive." "This is where Jean Harlow's husband killed himself." "This is where Clark Gable lives." Detie was happier than I had ever seen her, feeling that she was seeing life in the sophisticated, fast lane.

After a night at a San Francisco hotel, we began looking for an apartment. The first landlady we encountered would not rent to two men. The second, Mrs. Schwab, managed a building on Post Street, a few blocks behind the St. Francis Hotel. She had a small apartment to rent. It didn't have a view but she had no qualms about two men sharing it. She put a cot in the kitchen for Detie. Mrs. Schwab was to become a good and faithful friend.

While Edwin went off to accept his job, Detie and I explored the "city by the bay," shopped for food, and prepared the evening meal. She enjoyed going out for a drink after Edwin returned from work, but soon it was time for her to return to Charleston. We said goodbye at the railroad station.

Having finished my novel, I sent it off to meet the deadline for the Dodd-Mead *Red Book* contest. It was much too short and probably not suitable for the competition, but I thought I might get a reaction which would be of value before sending it off somewhere else. When it returned, I sent it to Doubleday, which also returned it. This was the last time I sent it out. I had, meantime, one of my first major poetry acceptances with *Harper's Bazaar* for "Betrayal."

Completing the novel, I realized that it was time for me to look for work. I went down to the Civil Service office, took a typing examination, and two weeks later was told to report to the very finance office where Edwin was employed. These types of strange coincidences continued throughout our life together. I was even given a desk next to his, a sort of a forerunner of the life we were to lead later, side by side.

Everyone knows of the beauties of San Francisco. In those days, it was a quiet and inexpensive city with many good eating places and friendly bars within our budget. Although there were some bars known for attracting homosexuals, we didn't know of any.[1] There was a bar, 150 feet long, not far from our apartment, where we felt comfortable among people who seemed to be the working poor. Drinks were ten cents, and we could speculate about the lives of the other customers.

We also went to Finocchio's, which was billed as having the "world's greatest female impersonators."[2] It was crowded, as usual, and most of the patrons were heterosexual couples on a sightseeing binge. The young men were beautiful as women, and the older ones, usually plump and homely beneath excessive make-up, were seasoned professionals, especially in the field of burlesque. They were more popular than the younger ones.

When we weren't working on weekends, we explored the city, sometimes walking across the exciting Golden Gate Bridge or taking the leisurely ferry to Sausalito across the bay. I particularly remember one Sunday morning when we set out for Golden Gate Park with only a Stone

Mountain Memorial fifty-cent piece for transportation or anything else. The conductor refused to take the unusual coin and made us get off. A nearby grocer was intrigued by the coin and said that, though we might be conning him, he thought it interesting enough to give us regular currency for it. We took the next street car and had enough for return fare and ice-cream cones. On that visit to the park we noticed obvious cruising and were amused by the subtlety or lack of it in the approaches.

Except for Washington, I had never lived anywhere that had as many good second-hand bookstores as San Francisco. We spent many hours on Saturdays searching them out and browsing, sometimes buying books we felt we could not live without. I believe the germ of the idea of opening a bookstore one day may have developed from the experiences we shared exploring these, for the most part, grubby, overcrowded book stacks. But we never spoke of such an eventuality.

One day I received a letter from Dorothy Heyward telling me that one of my plays, *The Game*, was being considered for the prize in the playwriting competition that was an annual event at the Dock Street Theater. The decision of the judges would be based on my availability to come back to Charleston to work on the play as it went into rehearsals. Of course, there was no way that I could interrupt my life at this point, the draft perhaps not too far down the road, my time with Edwin in jeopardy. I wrote back, without any regrets, of my decision not to return to Charleston.

I continued to write, though, and Edwin joined the Book of the Month Club, mainly to get the free edition of Proust. I was reading Walden for the first time. I found many points of agreement between Thoreau and myself, but living alone has never been a satisfactory mode of life for me. I require at least one person to share my fits of despondency or joy. With a companion, Walden Pond would be ideal.

One late Sunday morning, December 7, we were listening to a classical music radio station, while I began preparing a grits and bacon brunch. Suddenly, an announcer broke into the music, describing the Japanese attack on Hawaii and our fleet at Pearl Harbor. Edwin and I listened to the news all afternoon. We remained during the evening listening to San Francisco authorities urging us to stay indoors, to be ready for a possible attack. We found something to cover our two windows to prevent light from guiding the Japanese bombers to the city.

That evening, we began to talk about our futures in the armed services. We both knew that we would never be able to kill an enemy face to face. But, the issue of our homosexuality or that we might not see one another for a long time never occurred to us.

The Navy seemed the most attractive alternative. Four months later, we became apprentice seamen in the Naval Reserve and were placed on inactive duty. We sent our books and the few items we wanted to keep to Charleston. On April 13, we set out by train, then bus, then another train to the U.S. Naval Training Station in San Diego, where we were to remain with about 30,000 other men until May 28.

Although we were living a new and utterly different sort of life, it soon became quite monotonous. The most unpleasant part of this life was waiting, at which we spent most of our time. The first week was something of a nightmare, with inoculations, issuance of clothing and sea bags, along with four moves into different barracks, a great deal of waiting for food that was plentiful but tasteless, unless you liked beans. Edwin was in the downstairs section of our barracks. From my upstairs corner there was a fine view of the harbor, ships, and city with hills at our back. We were always cold (even with two heavy wool blankets), and the sound of coughing was heard all night, drowning out the pleasanter noise of men snoring. After about three weeks, Edwin developed pneumonia, from which he recovered so rapidly that the day he was dismissed from the dispensary he was scrubbing floors again.

I think that my experience as a knob at The Citadel had prepared me well for this sort of military life, as I found the routines through which we were put easier than I had expected. We were among much younger men, some of them almost children, with spirits lively enough to suit a Martha Raye. We were also amused by our lax company commander and his handsome seventeen-year-old recruit assistant, who one day told all of us, "You all got to keep quiet 'till I done speak my piece." He would tell us to get into our "Duncan greens." It was difficult to have much respect for a system that put such a man in charge of 160 men.

About a month into our stay at the base, we were given intelligence and aptitude tests. It was a farce. The people who knew little copied from those whom they thought knew more. While awaiting the results, I worked in the company office helping the Yeoman, which exempted me from guard or cleaning duty and most of the drills. Several days later, Edwin and I took the examination in typing for Yeoman. Edwin was nervous and didn't pass, but he misunderstood the examining officer and followed me into the room where Yeomen were being processed—and became a Yeoman too! This translated into sixty dollars a month and office work.

We also experienced our first leave. Edwin and I attended a flower show in La Jolla. We arrived in warm fettle right at the library where the show was held in the garden. The ample bosomed ladies greeted us warmly and escorted us through rows of drooping roses, long wilted. We then visited Edwin's family friends. We returned to La Jolla on our next leave, arriving in time for midday dinner at the best hotel we could find clothed in our best whites. We ate on a patio where bougainvillea, roses, geraniums, hibiscus, and other flowers were in full bloom. As we were finishing our meal, the waitress told us that "a gentleman would like to buy your lunch, if you don't mind." We were rather embarrassed but agreed to allow him that pleasure. We spent the afternoon wandering around the town, along the cliffs, where nasturtiums were mingling with ice plants. The water was a wonderful blue. It was difficult to remember that we were at war. After a lazy afternoon, we returned to the hotel, lunch money in pocket, and had another feast. Jack Benny was sitting at the next table.

Often during our six weeks in San Diego we received packages of goodies from family or from my friend, George Scheirer. These were shared, as was the custom, with our friends among the sailors. One day, after his sixth haircut, Edwin came in with news from Carson's mother "Bebe," that our friends, Edward N. and Bob, had called on her and that they were becoming good acquaintances. Bob was then stationed at Fort Benning. When Carson returned from New York, she, too, became a good friend of Bob and Edward, who called on the Smiths often, usually bringing gifts of records or liquor.

On May 26, our company went through a radical change. Men were being sent out in all directions: Jacksonville, Florida, Chicago, College Station, Texas, Oxford, Ohio, leaving only about forty-five in our company. Two days later, Edwin and I found ourselves on Treasure Island. It was a site actually created for the 1939 World's Fair by dredging fill from the Bay and named after the Stevenson novel. Peering from the island's shore to San Francisco, I thought about our civilian life, just a few months earlier, living at Mrs. Schwab's building on Post Street. Her only remaining son had been killed that very month in a plane taking off for Panama. The distance from San Francisco, in both time and miles, now seemed far away.

At this base, there seemed to be an oversupply of Yeoman and Storekeepers, and they were hard put to keep us busy. I often helped peel thousands of potatoes which Edwin and others poured from 100-pound sacks into a machine that removed some of the skins. After two weeks, we were reassigned.

There was no place to which we could go to become intimate, but we remembered that a gay young man in our former office had talked about a Turkish bath that he attended. We went there one night. I was very nervous about going in. However, the friendly and erotic ambience calmed me, and, after a steam bath, we found a small room to which we retired. We went back the next week.

Edwin was sent to the Section Base at Monterey and I to Morro Bay, about 150 miles south of his base. From Morro Bay there was a spectacular view, when it was not obscured by fog, of the great rock, the ocean, the brown hills, and sand bars. The village also had a fine drugstore at which I sometimes indulged myself in a chocolate sundae, but the eating places were terrible, as was our base food. I was assigned to scullery, which didn't bother me although handling garbage bags never appealed to me. But, it could have been so much worse. We were afraid we were all going to be sent out on patrol boats, usually converted yachts which were not always comfortable in a rough sea. Any prolonged rocking motion upset me, which probably sounds strange given our choice of armed services.

Given their excess, Yeomen had been sent up and down the coast to fill in at other duties. Poor Edwin, though, was assigned to the radio room in Monterey. He was at the mercy of flashing lights and strange sounds without any instructions. In time, he became used to his duties though his bad hearing made it difficult for him to understand speech, and he often had to call someone to listen in for him. Such were the inscrutable ways of the Navy.

Toward the end of June, I had a liberty weekend and traveled to Monterey. The trip there was the first time I had hitchhiked as a sailor, and I was pleased to find that one did not even have to lift a finger to catch a ride if one was in uniform—and the drivers were better than the one we had encountered on our trip to Key West.

Edwin and I spent most of the time in Carmel, glowing with riotous flowers and a very blue bay. When we stopped at the United Services Organization (USO), we received free tickets to a concert by Menuhin, who played, among other compositions, the Franck Sonata in A Major, a favorite of both of ours.

The weeks passed at Morro Bay. Amidst tirades of the commissary steward, the marine mess cook, and the old Filipino cook, I would often go to sit in the mess hall to write. At my back was the fog, rolling in and veiling the dredging action, completely obscuring the great rock. Edwin said I should write a poem about the Rock, like Hart Crane's Bridge, but I didn't care to attempt that in those times of mental inactivity. I did, however, use that time to write to George as well as to Edward and Bob. They, in turn, wrote to me as well as to Edwin. It was a correspondence that continued throughout the war years.

Edwin loved getting mail, made friends easily, and adjusted to any duties well. His willingness to help out in any situation made him stand out in the company of other sailors.

When not writing or on scullery duty, I often found myself reading. For a time I was reading *Black Lamb and Gray Falcon*, Rebecca West's fascinating work on Yugoslavia. Whenever I needed refreshment of the spirit I turned to it as it really is a profession of faith. One time, a Filipino mess attendant, who bunked near me, came up to chat. Pete was a delightful character. His English was not good, but it was filled with a poetic quality which revealed real imagination. "Why are you sad? Have you a sentiment in your heart for someone who is far away?" I dared not talk to him about Edwin, though I would have liked to have done so.

At another time, he asked, "Do you know what love is? It is the torment of one; the felicity of two; the sweet amity of three." He had read that somewhere, I supposed, but it fit well my feelings toward Edwin. Like other couples and lovers, our lives had dramatically changed. But, since

Figure 6.1 Edwin and John together in the Navy.

we were men, we had been able to serve together during the first few months. We were, I suppose, lucky in that way, and, although certainly not the only homosexuals in the Navy, probably two of the few who were a couple.[3] Would we, I wondered, be able to be together when the war was over and live our lives in the peace and harmony we had known before?

Pete interrupted my thinking as he sat on my bunk. He gave me a snapshot of himself and wrote on the back, "When you are in the middle of your sorrow, look at this photo and comfort yourself. That's me, Pete." I carried that snap with me for years.

The highlight of my time at Morro Bay was the arrival of Topie Johnson at nearby San Luis Obispo. I met her for dinner and a lesson in the hula, the noise of which caused someone in the next room to bang the walls. I decided it was time for me to return to base. We were not to see each other again until we were eighty. While visiting my nephew's family in Indianapolis, we decided to drive to Dayton to visit Topie and her husband, former head of a college history department. We had lunch with them at their home after talking non-stop, covering some of the events in our lives during the intervening fifty years. It was as though we were back in our younger years, reminiscing about Edwin, Carson, and the many years when we had only had greeting-card contact. This was our last time together.

We never knew from one day to the next when we would move or be moved. Toward the end of July, word came to the base that, as there were too many Yeomen in the Navy, some of us would have to change ratings. Among those offered, Radioman seemed the most suited to me and Edwin as it required typing, at which we were both proficient. I got in touch with Edwin immediately. We both decided to choose that rating. A few days later, word came that those going to radio school would go to one of four places. There was no time to call Edwin but I knew that he would choose the University of Colorado at Boulder. I chose Boulder, therefore, and, when I was able to telephone him, learned that he had chosen it, too. Thus, on the second of August I departed Morro Bay for my new assignment at the Naval Training Station.

Edwin's group joined us as we went up the coast before heading by train for Denver and on to Boulder. At one point in the Denver area, his group was switched to another train, which arrived before mine. He had been assigned a room and roommate, but I, perhaps because my name was Zeigler and the last man needing quarters, was given a room of my own. Once again, Edwin and I were together and could be together intimately.

7   Colorado Schooling

Attending radio school at the University of Colorado in Boulder with Edwin allowed us to have university privileges. The campus was beautiful in full summer, with green grass, towering aspens, great mountains, and far-flung plains. The hill that rose over the west was, by day, much like a Cezanne as I looked out my vine-covered dormitory window with birds chattering away in the morning like sailors before code class.

Our only duty was to go to school from eight until five, followed by an hour of athletics. We listened to code with earphones four hours each day, then had two hours of procedure and another two hours of typing. The better we performed in school, the more choice of duty we would have after we finished the course, so we worked hard. If anyone failed, they would become seamen!

We could not believe our good luck in being together. Most evenings we would go to the library to choose books from its splendid collection. Classical music played in one area with copies of Picasso, Gauguin, and Cezanne hung on the walls.

In many ways, though, Edwin and I were opposites. He was always ready for any exertion, while I was inclined to easy forms of exercise. He wanted to see the view from the tallest mountain, while I am content to walk in the valley and look up. He disliked possessions while I am happy among familiar objects. And yet we were strangely suited as companions. He got me out of an old habit of brooding introspection, cheered me up, and kept me moving about in the various realms of nature. Edwin had a solitary nature whereas I love company. He was happiest when discovering a wild flower he had never seen; I, in discovering something new in my friends.

During two weekends, we took trips into the mountains. There were thirty-six hours of uninterrupted delight. By hitchhiking we ran into all sorts of good people. We inevitably rode in crowded cars overflowing with children and luggage. We held the children or the blankets or the boxes while learning a bit about ranching, or mining, or some other interest of our hosts. But most of all, I enjoyed the friendliness of these people. There was a short and enormously stout mother and her going-to-be-that-way daughter of sixteen and a childish fourteen-year-old son. They sat on the back seat, teasing, screaming, and whispering good naturedly, unmindful of us. The father—good, poor, and hardworking—listened and must have been enjoying it for they teased him, too. When the car seemed to hesitate about a steep grade, they all laughed with joy. When we said goodbye, it was with a feeling of sadness that we would never see each other again.

We took the road over 12,000 feet, high across great tundra, where ice banks ten feet thick sloped to melting pools, with streams that led to the beginnings of forests, sparkling in the afternoon light. It was forty-five miles from the village of Estes Park, from which we had left, across the mountain, to Grand Lake. We spent the night there and went to a tavern dance, where I drank more than I should have. Everyone was buying us drinks, and we danced with the local girls, talked, and the evening was merry. I regretted the drinking on Sunday, though, when I was hitchhiking again to Idaho Springs and Central City, a town untouched by anything but time with shops that seemed to have been deserted for half a century.

In September, we spent a couple of nights in Denver at the posh Brown Palace Hotel to participate in a weekend word-game contest, which included spelling. Our first snowfall came during that stay, and the spelling contest brought me a watch, as winner, with Edwin coming in second. He had spelt "Novocain" with an "e" at the end, which is shown in some dictionaries. I think we should have tied.

It was about this time that our code program was accelerated to six hours a day. We all became rather jumpy and nervous at the intensity of our studies, which were monotonous and boring. Sometimes I felt that a well-placed scream would serve to relieve me temporarily. Some did throw down their earphones or slam a chair against a wall, or utter some loud and rude serviceable syllable.

One Saturday, Edwin decided that we needed a little new excitement: I should ride a horse. We went to a nearby stable where I mounted the animal awkwardly, took a few very uncomfortable turns around the corral, and heard Edwin suggest that we take off for the hills. I dismounted. Edwin howled. As I headed back to campus he took off for a glorious afternoon alone. Even at that age, I am afraid I did not have the patience to learn many more things, preferring to cultivate those pursuits in which I had already got a start. It was about then that we began to notice how often three of the handsomest men in our class went off for weekends with an older bachelor professor of English. We looked at them with renewed interest but never asked questions.

In late October, we had our first big snow, about two feet. Edwin went wild and threw snowballs at all the passersby. On a Sunday, we walked up Boulder canyon, and the creek was running noisily, icicles beginning to melt. The air was exhilarating, and we shouted with joy at just being alive. After some miles we were picked up by two college students in an old car. As we approached the large lake at Nederland, we could see the real mountains, almost covered with snow, rising higher and higher in the distance. We had a drink in the Silver Dollar Tavern, and, shortly afterward, there was a recital by Alexander Brailowsky, who played brilliantly a long and varied program that included a group of Chopin works and Beethoven's Appassionata Sonata. Almost every night we would be in the music room of the library, but it was a special treat to hear music live from the first row!

We had colds for weeks, but Edwin's was the more uncomfortable as it interfered with his practice of code. About that time, I heard from a woman's college in Alabama asking what royalty I would expect if they performed my play *At Home with Miss Glover*. I told them "anything," but nothing ever came of this. I did, however, write two or three pieces of new verse. I picked up *Swann's Way* while waiting for meals, or for Edwin to come by for some reason or other, or in the few minutes between coming in from town and lights out.[1] I have never enjoyed Proust more. I suppose that is the way he should be read, in short doses. Perhaps when I was reading him and feeling slightly unwell and thus filled with the depression of lassitude, I was just ripe for Proust, whose unhealthiness permeates his work. So, I felt for the time being like one who has played in the park with Gilberte and Himself, or who has visited Odette with Swann, or who has been at Combray in the garden reading.

Finally, we finished our schooling. Assignments were handed out based upon standing in the class and choice. There were only twelve assignments to Alaska, and, as I had done well, I got the second assignment there. Edwin's beginning deafness kept him from doing well, and eleven places had been filled before he finally got the twelfth. It had always been a dream of Edwin's to go to Alaska.

On November 18, we left for Bremerton Navy Yard, across from Seattle, for further assignment. It was mostly a time of waiting, hanging around the barracks, going occasionally into Seattle in the rain on the ferry. One day, I helped three nuns with their suitcases as they boarded the ferry, then took the bags off when we docked. One of the nuns called out to a cab, which had to be shared with passengers already seated, while the other two tried to make me accept a tip. As I continued to refuse and to hurry away, they followed me, calling, skirts flying as I vanished into the distance. I sometimes wonder what the onlookers thought I had done to those sweet ladies.

After three weeks in Bremerton, we sailed for Kodiak in an overcrowded ship. I was grossly seasick. It was probably the most physically miserable time of my life for it lasted a week. The rough sea in stormy winter weather did not bother Edwin. He brought me his fruit from breakfast and ice cream from the canteen and tried to cheer me up when I was not in the latrine.

Our first view of Alaska, on the first anniversary of the bombing of Pearl Harbor, was of a land of spectacular beauty, mountains and sea contrasting sharply: Two men on a ridge stood out like giants. Our barracks were new, so new that the hot water had not been connected. The room was warm, and we braved the icy water available to get some of the week's grime off, never having removed our life jackets on the voyage. The food was plentiful—and unlike that in California—tasty. We particularly enjoyed our brisk walks to breakfast, some distance from the quarters, in starlight or softly falling snow. It had a romantic charm, and it satisfied Edwin's dream, at least for the time being.

Well, he was about to see more of it than Kodiak, for the day before Christmas he was sent to Cape Chiniak, where he would remain for a year and three months with a handful of other men, not always the same, enduring many hardships at first but later settling into a routine that gave him time in good weather for exploring the region and its flora. In the desert of high-school tomfoolery in which we had been living, he had given me balance and tolerance, a peace of mind I had never had before, and I wondered gravely how I would get through the rest of the war years.

8   Yakutat

> The rain is in the wind,
> And in the mirrorless
> Long day that never ends.
> It drops upon the hemlocks
> Or it beats upon the rocks
> Where the bay bends
> And the slim gray birds sit motionless
> Like flowers in a garden, thinned.
> The rain is in the wind,
> And in the passionless
> Gray faces of the men.
> It offers neither docks
> Nor seas, only the rocks,
> And spongy moss within the flooded fen.
> It binds with loneliness
> The sailors pacing in the land's wind.
> Rain in Alaska

The plane seemed to swim down through the clouds. Turning, we saw at a distance great Mount Saint Elias, with the awesome Malaspina Glacier spreading from its base to the sea. Soon we were over land, the evergreens standing like grass in the snow and ice of Alaska. To our left was the horseshoe shape of Yakutat Bay, a few houses scattered on its northern shore. We wheeled, and the grass became trees and came up to meet us. We touched the scar on the landscape, the runway, and, purring in godlike precision, came to a stop near the small hangar. The plane left almost at once, its mission to deliver me to this spot having been accomplished. In no time, a truck came rattling around the corner of the hangar. It took me to the naval base I would share with thirty-five other landlocked sailors for the following year and a half. The date was January 19, 1943.

Figure 8.1 John at Yakutat, Alaska.

After a pleasant welcome in the office of the Executive Officer, I was taken to the small cabin I would share with the Radio Chief, who had been in the Navy for many years. I was to escape often from his tobacco chewing and spitting to the Quonset hut where the other seamen lived. The large building that was called the Radio Shack also held the other offices for the four officers on the base.

On my second day, I was approached by a twenty-year-old radioman who had been at Boulder. He grabbed his crotch and said, "Don't you want it, Zeigler?" I told him to shut up. He made the same approach the next day and got the same answer. In a few days, I noticed that he was going off into the woods with the cook. That was the only sexual activity I ever noticed on the base.

During the evenings, I might play a game of dominos in the mess hall, read old copies of *Time* and *Newsweek*, or go over to the army base by truck to see a movie. It was a beautiful ride in the late afternoon, with the evergreens forming a long avenue and the snow all about. I'd also pass my free time reading. At that time, I was reading *Wuthering Heights* again. One of the seamen I spent time with in the Quonset hut was great fun to be around. We talked of poetry, and he usually had a Shakespeare play with him. Although he read psychology and philosophy, his knowledge of them seemed somewhat shaky. Since he didn't have much education, he admired those who did, and he was really starved for affection. His parents were newspaper folks so there was much we had in common.

Toward the end of January, on my Sunday off, I made my first visit into the village of Yakutat. It wasn't a very good day to go for the large store was closed, and the little store in the white settlement, known as Old Yakutat, did not offer much. The only things I could buy were some postcards. The population, though, was predominantly Native American, and they lived in little frame houses not unlike the sharecropper's cabins in my native South. In one window I noticed a few artificial flowers and at some windows were curtains. Eventually, I would learn the names of some of the Indians: Lame Jack, Yakutat Charley, Slow Sam, Dry Bay Charley, Bing Bong, Chock Yock, Sitka Ned, Yataga John, Iteena Skoo—people I would talk with from time to time.

Throughout our times apart in the service, Edwin and I frequently (along with George and others) exchanged letters. I always signed mine to Edwin, "your cousin," since all letters were subject to military censors who would read my letters to him. In one of the early letters to Edwin, I wrote:

> Don't you miss music? When we hear it again, how will it be to learn everything again? Sometimes I find myself singing some aria and it seems more beautiful than it ever did before. Perhaps it is a good thing to get away from those things we love, at times, so that we can come

to them again in a fresher spirit and never again, perhaps, take them for granted.[1]

Writing vaguely enough to avoid suspicions but specific enough to communicate was an interesting challenge. The closest letter that ever got into a gay discussion was when Bo, my former lover from Washington, wrote to say that our good friends, Ed and Bob, had come up to his mother's house after Christmas. "I like Bob very much," Bo wrote. "From all reports Bob is leading Ed a merry dance."[2] In a letter to Edwin reporting this, I said:

> I hope that it is only talk that Bo has heard. I remember that when they first went to Washington I wondered if something might not come up of that nature, but I thought, too, that they were both rather satisfied with the way things were. I don't want to ever look at anyone else.[3]

I also heard regularly from George. He sent me a fable he had written which was very touching, and I often sent him short stories or poetry I was working on. Seldom was our correspondence explicit, though, in one letter toward the end of my stay in Alaska, he closed by saying:

> Me, I cannot find it in my heart to blame anyone for not liking me. In fact, truly I cannot make a good case for myself at all.... There shall continue many nights when, after all is quiet, and dark, and restful, George will invoke health and strength for the mind and spirit and body of Edwin and John.

I relayed this to Edwin in a letter that was taken to Seattle for mailing by a friend going on leave. I wrote: "You will notice that he did not say mind*s*, spirit*s*, bodie*s*." I added, "I was very frank in expressing my feelings for you (without admitting anything). I think that next to you and Edward N., I feel more affection for him than anyone else." Finally, in this letter that escaped the prying censor's eyes, I told Edwin not to worry "about anything I might write to him; and do not think that I will take advantage of my situation and write letters of this nature again.... All shall be as before in this correspondence, which seems, at best, only a halfway thing."[4]

My situation and relative freedom from the censors, when I could get someone to take letters on leave, was different from Edwin's who found it unbearable to the point of not wanting to write anymore. "Letters are important," I told him:

> Your letters are important to me. I must know what is happening to you, even what you are reading, what you think about what you read,

if you receive my letters, and all the little things that can mean so much in times like these.... Your unhappiness is mine, too.... Edwin, when things are bad, can't you think of that time that will come when we will be working together at something we like?[5]

In one letter, George quoted Somerset Maugham, saying that the greatest of all war work is working with impossible people.[6] I had to agree with Maugham's observations. Over the course of the eighteen months I spent at Yakutat, enlisted men and officers would come and go. There were a few, however, who were quite memorable. Chief Long, with whom I shared a cabin, was a pleasant easygoing fellow who was a bit old maidish but chewed tobacco, spitting his juice into his "goop" can that he carried around. He carved ivory chessman and bracelets, puttered around with a saw and hammer, and played jigs and hornpipes on his violin. Sometime he would get out his saxophone, which he could barely play. One evening, I called out from my bunk, where I had gone to be with *The Red Badge of Courage*, and asked if he knew Camptown Races. He did. He sat on a bunk and played for an hour. I decided it was politic to stay awake.

Sometimes I would go to movies with Keim. He was just twenty and studying all the time, trigonometry and such, hoping to go to college after the war. His father was a Lieutenant Commander in the Navy, a doctor. Perhaps that is why Keim complained far less than most. When we first met, he had already been up there for more than a year after joining the Navy at the age of seventeen. He called me the brain, but later, as he got to know me better, it was anything but that. But he liked to walk so went along with me on some of my fieldtrips—although I wished Edwin had been there instead to relieve my ignorance of the plants and fauna.

My best friend on the base was eighteen-year-old Eric, who, as a youngster, had been sent to Providence, Rhode Island, to stay with relatives and escape the bombings in England. Because he was a little awkward and somewhat different from the American sailors, he was often the butt of good-natured but hurting comments. He was thought to be not very bright. I soon learned that he had a natural intelligence that was above the average. When I visited the Quonset hut, I would often sit on his bed, and he would cuddle up to me, secure in the safety that my presence kept him, for no one ever made fun of him when I was around.

There was nothing sexual in our closeness on his bunk, and no one thought anything of it. We often walked together, and he liked to ask me questions about various matters. I was delighted for him when he took the test for Storekeeper Third Class and passed with splendid results. After our base closed, we kept in touch and twice just missed each other in cities through which we were passing. After the war, I saw him once in New York when my aunt and I were there on holiday. He was out of the service and employed in some mechanical work.

Unlike civilian life, getting mail (like everything else) in the military and during wartime was difficult. Edwin's letters would usually come in batches along with a mail sack of letters from my family as well as those from my Washington friends, with George being the most frequent correspondent. It would be like Christmas as I was reading letters and opening packages. There was often candy such as benne brittle, nuts, and tins of oatmeal or Bentzen cookies but sometimes the homemade stuff had spoiled. Wool socks, razor blades, magazines, and books were particularly appreciated.

One of the magazines I received in March was *Harper's Bazaar*, which featured a story by Carson. During my stay in Alaska, she would publish two books, which I read while on base. "I believe," I wrote Edwin, "Carson is a lonely spirit, always seeking a hearth where she can feel at home. I can understand that, for it took me almost thirty years to find what spelled fireside and an end to restlessness."[7]

There, too, was an occasional letter from Carter. Early on, he wrote that he and Perks had had physicals. But then the thirty-eight-year age limit went into effect, and they were exempted for the present. Carter celebrated—but then he celebrated all the time. Months later, I received a set of snapshots from Perks. He had the happy habit of describing his pictures so there was no need for me to comment on them. The night view of Connecticut Avenue taken from his apartment's window, just above mine, was great. Another snap of Perks lying on the grass was where we used to pitch our blankets and sleep out near Harper's Ferry. We continued to exchange letters and cards.

As Edwin and I settled down into our own routines several hundred miles apart, we exchanged ideas about going in on a farm when the war was over.

> I was thinking the other day of the fact that, since the peregrinations which began in May 1941, we have never had those belongings of ours—books, records, etc.—with us. If we wanted a book, we had to hitchhike to Santa Fe or go looking in a lending library on Polk Street. If we wanted to hear music, we had to take what was being offered on the power-company program. No place was quite home, was it? And that is what a farm should be, a place for growing enough to live on, a cow, some chickens (Lenny and George in Of Mice and Men). Perhaps some pigs for fall butchering. And wouldn't you like the beginnings of a nursery? Not one for children![8]

I wrote to the Agricultural Department for any material they had on fruit and nut trees in the coastal area of South Carolina. Peggy was saving cheese glasses along with other odds and ends for our farm. Later, when I received *Apples East of the Mississippi*, I devoured it. I asked Edwin, "Why does it take those things so long to begin bearing? I long for fruit trees of my own."

Edwin and I religiously deposited earnings into our bank accounts for a future dream together. This got me through each day, hoping it would not simply become a pipe dream. As the months wore on, plans for the farm grew more elaborate. I proposed to Edwin that we also open an eating place on the farm to be called The Farmhouse which would be open just for dinner or on Sundays.

As Edwin and I exchanged ideas, I finally put to words my reasons for returning to Charleston and engaging in farm activity, while trying to see Edwin's perspective:

> Thomas Wolfe and I . . . have a similar feeling about the places from which we come. . . . The Lowcountry means more to me than any other place I suppose. I love the rivers and marshes but I hate the heat. . . . [B]eing out in the country would remove the proximity to the Charleston people which might prevent much work. . . .
>
> After the war, I will be in no mood to write for some time. If I went to San Francisco or Santa Fe it would be nice but it would not be for writing. In Charleston, Santa Fe, San Francisco it took me a couple of months after getting there to settle down to writing. Say we went either to SF or Santa Fe for six months or a year, I would be fiddling around, spending all my savings. Say, instead, that we started right out finding a place (leaving out, now, any idea of its locality). We would do some building and that would take some time but we would have it after we built it. Then we could begin gradually to do some planning, get chickens, etc. If we didn't want to do anything much for a while, it would be all right. And the money we would be spending somewhere else on rent, etc. we would be putting in a house and some land.
>
> I know that farming on any scale requires a lot of time and hard work. I don't think it necessary to do it on any big scale. I know there are seasons when there isn't a whole lot to do and I think that those seasons would be time enough for any writing I might do. The whole thing boils down to this: I don't want to work in any damn office any more. I don't think you do either. I know you like to work in the outdoors. There must be something we can do together. . . .
>
> You say I'm nuts about a farm. I am only talking about that because I can't think of anything better. . . . You must not think that I am set on Charleston or on a farm. Your own ideas interest me more than my own and I am anxious to hear some of them.[9]

We continued to go back and forth on what we might do after the war, talking at one point of opening an inn rather than farming or about "a small farm not farmed."

When I was not working, thinking about our future, or reading, I'd sometimes walk along the rocky beach or on the path that was just within the forest, on a slight rise above the sea's edge. The walks helped to get the dits-dahs noise out of my head after hours on the radio. There was a rock, I remember, that rose from the path, which followed the bay at a height, and on top of the rock were several trees. Perpendicular on all sides but facing the sea, the fifteen-foot rock had footholds. It was isolated and charming—a place, I wrote to Edwin, that was especially suited "for lovers. I am not sure that one should live with grandeur constantly. You take it for granted. But charm lasts. . . ."[10] What didn't last were my walks after I saw fresh bear dung on the path.

On one such walk, I ran into an elderly man with a couple of dogs. He dropped his knapsack and obviously wanted to talk. "I'm Danny Lane, and you'll be seeing a lot of me when the salmon start running," he began. He had lived in Alaska for fifteen years. "Alaska's an old man's country. If I was younger I'd be back in the States or in the Army. Up here a man can get along without being beholden to anyone. A sourdough's the freest man in the world." He had to go, he said, but then added: "So long, young man, when you get too old for 'em just come back to Alaska!"

I recalled some of the local history, visualizing the proud and angry Indians of an earlier time putting out from this shore in their long and sturdy canoes, the warriors among them wearing the helmets, shields, and breastplates of war. Along that same curve of beach, with the waters perhaps as still and blue as today, the Indians had once brought the heads of their Russian enemies, by whom they were once subdued, slain in a final decisive fight, and they had placed them on pikes that followed the contour of the beach—a savage warning to future intruders.

After being stationed at Yakutat for a few months, it seemed as though there was just nothing more to say in my letters home. It seemed as though I repeated myself endlessly, and I knew the letters were being passed around anyway. Chief Long, who had a wife and two children, thought letters were simply a waste of time and would just as soon not receive any mail. However, Edwin's letters were never trivial. Even if he felt he had nothing to say, I wanted him to write whenever he could.

The monotony and isolation at the camp were difficult. One evening, I heard the tail end of Beethoven's Sixth then switched the dial and heard the beginning. It was a little like being home again with some of my dearest possessions about me. Closing my eyes, I could imagine a hot summer evening in that hot attic when Edwin and I shared scotch (I don't think it was rum) with our shirts peeled. As good as those days were, they grew into something even better, so I told myself when depression hit me, that even those lackluster months will lead to a far better time.

Many people disliked being stationed in Alaska. One soldier I talked to told me fifty-four fellows in his regiment had blown their brains out in a year's time. As time passed, though, I liked the small base and its isolation; Edwin though grew unhappier as our Alaskan stay wore on.

Although I tried to keep my letters to Edwin frequent and upbeat, there were times I lapsed into melancholy:

> I don't know what happens to time. Frequently there is an intolerable ache for the past and longing for the future, but one learns to wait and to be thankful for memories which contain so much to think about with pleasure. How I pity some people, when I turn to things I have seen and heard in the last few years. To Asheville at midnight; to apple juice drunk all night in Gatlinburg; to the late twilight in the forest below Clingman's Dome, when everything was so unreal as to make the place seem like something in a dream . . . ; To warm sun and beautiful waters of Key West; the little rock garden, the apple trees, the stream at Tesuque; the square of Santa Fe, the brown hills outside San Francisco, the Bridge, the redwoods, the view from the palace. The fun at El Nidos, at F's. Central City, Nederlands, Estes Park, and so many other places.[11]

I supposed the thing that annoyed me most in the camp was hearing others gripe. We had it so easy compared to most of the people in Europe and the South Pacific, and we grumbled about the stupidest things: mail delays, warm beer and poor chow, months to see a dentist. Monotony, though, was the greatest curse. I could walk in one direction and know most of the fallen trees and bushes by heart.

In the early months of Alaskan duty, I began to have poetry accepted by such publications as the *American Mercury*, *Lyric*, *New York Times*, and *Herald Tribune*. In January, I had one of the most encouraging days of my life. It began with a note from Doubleday recalling the fact that they had thought my novel, *By Slant and Twist*, promising. The editor asked if I had any work in progress. Next, there came a letter from a writer on the *New York Sun* saying that he had read my poem, "The Ermine," when it was printed in the *Sun* and liked it. Subsequently, he was at a meeting of the Poetry Society of America where the poet Leonora Speyer told him she had clipped "The Ermine" and read it to her poetry class at Columbia University. Later in the day, a letter came from the Armed Forces Service League informing me that I was one of the winners in its short-story and cartoon contest for servicemen. "Day Off" thus won a 100-dollar war bond and would be published in a volume to be called *Fighting Words*.[12] That was my happiest day at Yakutat.

Throughout the summer, Edwin's whereabouts were somewhat uncertain. As the weeks and months collapsed together, there was an occasional respite in my routine. There was a USO show at the army base. Friends and I went over early, hitchhiking. When we entered the canteen, Carol Winters, the dancer in the troupe of five, was there with the Master of Ceremonies. Carol was pert and vivacious. She began talking to us, and we got very friendly, especially after one of my friends learned that the other girl in the show, an accordionist, was an old friend from Pawtucket, with whom he used to play guitar. That "fixed everything up," so we invited the troupe over to dinner the next day. Carol sat with us. At a moment when I had a mouthful of food, she embraced and kissed me. The whole dining room burst into laughter. All eyes were on that table anyway. They tell me my ears got red. Six weeks later, I learned that Carol and a couple of others in the troupe were killed in a plane accident in Canada when they were returning home after doing ten months of shows.

Other USO shows came afterward, including one with Ingrid Bergman and Neil Hamilton, hero of the silents, where I was just six feet from the stage. All of the beauty, charm, and graciousness she seemed to have on the screen were multiplied when I saw her. Her voice as she sung Swedish folk songs was wonderful. Her eyes were bright, so full of life and so expressive. Her complexion was the sort you read about. She wore no makeup, no fingernail polish. Her hair was natural, growing back rapidly from *For Whom the Bell Tolls*. She was to have dinner with us that night, and I was going to do the honors at her table. But, her plans had been delayed, and she was late in arriving.

A couple of weeks before that plane crash, we had the first dance on our base. The log-hut recreation room had been completed, and it was opened for the dance. Twenty-eight ladies, Native Americans for the most part, from the village planned to attend, and, in preparation, I went with another seaman several miles into the woods to get decorations. We got many ferns and lupin, and pale Indian paintbrush. I put the ferns against the log beams and then made a centerpiece of floating yellow water lilies and pads with some small white flowers and green stuff around the rim of a large cooking pan. For music, we used an old Victrola with some good records. I danced just about every dance for over three hours.

The women, ranging in age from fourteen to sixty, were brought in a truck which let them out at the entrance to the hut. They lined up along a wall, we sailors on another. As the music began, we would rush to pick out the best dancers. One of them, about age forty, was an excellent dancer and my favorite partner. We hardly said more than a dozen words to each other. The truck awaited them at the door when the dance was over. There was to be no "hanky-panky" on the base!

The next evening, during my watch, a couple of fellows came down and told me that this woman wanted me to meet her. Of course, I didn't believe it at first and wouldn't yet except for the fact that one of these guys knew everyone in the village, had spent much time with the women, and was a rather honest friend of mine. But, we were sometimes forbidden to go to the village, and it was a good thing. I would have hated to have disappointed her as one of my friends had already slept with her. She must have liked my thinning hair.

Much later, I wrote to Edwin:

> I wish I were of a more gregarious nature so that I might get to know the people in the village better, especially the natives. I am particularly shy of the Indians, perhaps because I am so conscious of the ways in which their lives have been affected by us and others like us. . . . [13]

During that autumn of 1943, the prospects for taking leave seemed to increase. I wrote Edwin about the possibility of us getting leave at the same time to join up in San Francisco around the end of the year. Since letters between us took a month or more to be delivered (when they were received at all), I proposed to leave word for Edwin at Sand Point, in Washington State, about what I expected to do. In the event that there was no word there, then I would also leave word at the local YMCA. Once leaving Seattle, I planned to write another letter to the Y and suggested that Edwin follow the same procedure. If either of us got to San Francisco, the plan was to leave word with our Post Street landlady as well as the men's club in the square.

As it turned out, Edwin was able to respond by letter before Thanksgiving telling me he would not likely be able to take leave. I decided to stall taking leave as long as possible, hoping Edwin could work something out.

Near Christmas, leave policy was changed requiring eighteen months of service, which knocked all plans for a loop. As the days had gone by, I was counting on it more and more and was almost convinced that by some careful maneuvering Edwin and I might spend some time together. Six months longer seemed unbearable.

About this time, I sent Edwin a quotation from Montaigne that I loved:

> While the body is still supple, it should for that reason be bent to all fashions and customs. And provided his appetite and will can be kept in check, let a young man boldly be made first for all nations and companies even for dissoluteness and excess if need be.

In order to busy myself, I took on a couple of other projects. In August, I became the base postmaster. I didn't think it would come with any pay, although eventually it did. I always tried to maintain a pleasant face no matter how many times a day I was asked by the same person if he had any mail, no matter how many times I heard the same jokes about mail, no matter how many times a day I was asked to "sell me some stamps now," even though we were open just two hours a day, or to "wrap this package for me, please." I really did more business out of business hours than in. And, of course, I learned that if you have accommodated someone a dozen times but are busy at something else the thirteenth and cannot be accommodating, then you become a heel. And my being postmaster didn't hasten the mail service; the mail situation was still foul.

Another pet project that kept me going was getting a library started on the base. Before, the books had been kept in the room in which the

Master at Arms lived. Most hadn't felt like bothering him. You had to just about walk over his bed to examine the books. The peculiar nature of masters at arms also entered into the lack of interest in the books. My goal was to have a library open each evening with different fellows helping out. It would be the only quiet place available for reading and writing. It would also be a place to check out the classical records which the base had accumulated. That was the best way I could think of to see that they were cared for. If not, the fellows would have probably bit hunks out of them to see if there was any difference in the way "better" music tastes. It took five months before the library was open but there were close to 500 books and many magazines. The hours, though, were a problem even though I had several volunteers.

Being older than most of the enlisted men and choosing not to pursue a commission, which made me even more of an oddity, I sometimes served as sort of a liaison between the officers and the seamen. It wasn't that I was always busy, but it seemed like I was frequently imposed upon. Sometimes I felt like I was an information bureau set up by Gracie Allen. The radiomen eventually put up a big sign across one wall in the radio room, beneath the clock. It said: "Yes, we know the clock doesn't work. No, we don't know where Zeigler is." By now I had been elevated to Radioman Second Class.

About this time, I was not at all happy about having to assist in a war-bond drive on the base. By continual kidding, more than by salesmanship, I succeeded in doubling the quota, which I had set. It was the first time I had ever tried to sell anything. I disliked it intensely, afraid that I might be called upon for future such pleadings.

Christmas Eve began with gifts of Babe Ruths and Butterfingers from Commander Corbett, who had been a vice-president with the candy company. In the evening, we joined the officers in their quarters for eggnog and Christmas carols. Several of the older sailors had been given whiskey by a couple of the officers, mine being a fifth of bourbon. When we left, we shared our liquor and began dancing together. In no time, I was passed out on the floor, not having had a drink in over a year. My friends took me to my hut and put me to bed, where I slept until a hangover woke me in the morning, keeping me from Christmas dinner.

In January, I paid my first visit to a native home. Our pharmacist mate was looking for a woman who made moccasins. The woman, about fifty-five, was seated near a window sewing a bead design on a leather jacket. She was reserved but friendly and was soon telling us about the meaning of the eagle and whale designs. I could sense that she believed in the old ways and held a little to scorn the white man's knowledge of birds and animals. The Indian woman told of the time in their history when the Indians talked to the wild creatures and almost captured them with bare hands.

I asked her if I could return and spend an afternoon talking to her. She told me I would be very welcome. But, she was leaving soon for a month's hunting. She told me of Ingrid Bergman's visit to her to order several pairs of moccasins for her daughter, Pia. After leaving her, Bergman stopped at the village store and bought five sweaters for the woman's youngest grandchildren.

From this grandmother, I began to learn a little local lore and wrote to the library at Juneau for any information on neighboring Indians. They referred me to a guy named Hardy, who had been living for years at Yakutat and operated a small grocery. I visited him, and in just a few minutes he gave me quite a little information. I later told the postmistress that I had been told he knew quite a lot about the Indians. She retorted, "He ought to, he fathered most of them."

Furthering my interest, one Sunday afternoon, I was hiking and paused at a cemetery where many of the Indians were buried. Several men were digging a grave. I was curious about their funerals as I wanted to have an incident in a novel I was contemplating located at the cemetery. If I had only been less timid, I would have inquired of the men, who were friendly, and would have learned that the funeral was being held that afternoon. The Lutheran minister later told me something of the funeral, but of course that wasn't like being a witness to it. I began ordering books such as *Alaska Natives* and *The Modern Growth of the Totem Pole on the Northwest Coast*.

Most of my reading for pleasure was in re-reading some of Ellen Glasgow's splendid novels, especially *Vein of Iron* and her *Barren Ground*.[14] I had just received her newest work, *A Certain Measure*, which was about her creative-writing process. This book impressed me so deeply that I wrote to her, expressing my admiration and special interest, as an aspiring writer, in *A Certain Measure*. She responded, "I have always felt that a book, if it is worth reading once, is worth reading again." She invited me to visit her in Richmond. When I was in Richmond briefly, while stationed nearby and on my way out of the service, I didn't have the courage to knock on her door, though I passed her house a couple of times.

It was around January 26th that the most exciting event in my Yakutat stay occurred. At about ten at night, three ships were seen entering the bay. The Commanding Officer immediately stationed about a dozen sailors along the shore with rifles. I remembered that some time before we had received a radio message that three Russian freighters were heading to Seattle for repair. I got word to the Company Commander, and he sent a small boat out to greet the Russians.

The Russians were our allies, and I was eager to do my part in creating one world that would live in peace and harmony. I was driven next day to the dock, where one of the ships was berthed, with the intention of asking the seamen to come to our base for a movie that night. Several men and two women greeted me warmly. We settled down to a game of dominoes without being able to speak to each other. I was served brown bread and sardines but only ate the former. I could draw a truck and point to the clock but couldn't think of how to tell them we wanted to share a movie with them. Suddenly, I remembered a Russian film I had seen. I uttered, in what I thought was a brilliant Russian accent, *Alexander Nevsky*. "Ah, kino," they responded.

That night I returned to fetch them. They were slow in assembling, and one of my officers called and demanded that we hurry. I was so annoyed with him I spoke angrily about the necessity of being good hosts at a time when we went days without amusement. We went to the movies and afterward gave the men beer and the women hard candies that we rounded up. The men did some Russian dancing, and we returned them to their ship. I saw them again the next night at the army theater, and they came hurriedly over to me with warm embraces. The next day they were on their way to Seattle. For a while I felt much better about the world.

In the spring, Edwin and I began to correspond again about plans for the future. I asked him if he thought there was a place in a farmhouse for a totem pole. But we spent more time discussing plans for leave, as the time was approaching. I told him I thought we each should go home, perhaps taking the fifty-two-hour Portland-to-Chicago train together, or meeting in Chicago on the way down or back, or me simply flying from Seattle to Chicago perhaps meeting him on the day of his train arrival. Luckily, Mr. Corbett said he would clear me for leave anytime after June 2, and that all I needed to do was to tell him just when I wanted to go, even if it was on short notice. The plan then became for Edwin to let me know the moment he got to Seattle, since mail then only took two days to arrive in Yakutat, but I "suggested" he send a wire, which would get there the next day. We would then either meet up in Seattle, Chicago, Washington, or South Carolina.

We had not seen each other since December 24, 1942. Letters, if and when they arrived, were a poor substitute for his presence. I felt these lines from Donne applicable to us:

> Rend us in sunder; thou canst not divide
> Our bodies so, but that our souls are tied,
> And we can love by letters still and gifts,
> And thoughts and dreams; love never wanteth shifts.[15]

In one letter, I wrote to Edwin cryptically:

> My life did not really begin until about July 7, 1940 and I had more happiness in the years between then and December, 1942 than in all the years before. As long as those two years were a part of the past and a shadowing of the future, which I feel will be richer than anything that has gone before, the present does not matter.[16]

Writing another time, more clearly, I said: "We may be seeing each other. I can't believe it. I hope I have only changed for the better."[17]

June 2 came and went, and I was still in Yakutat. Edwin's leave was delayed but Mr. Corbett was ready to sign me out. On June 19, I wrote Edwin:

> It looks as though I won't be in the States before another month. . . . [Y]esterday the blow fell and my head is hanging on by a single nerve which is almost crying out to be severed. My leave is cancelled and I will have to proceed to Sitka with the rest of the bunch after we close down here. . . . Yesterday morning I completed my postal audit and had everything packed and was waiting as I thought the ship on which I might leave would come in yesterday. Then these guys appeared out of the blue and the station was up all night packing stuff to ship west.

There didn't seem to be any avenue of escape for me. In that same letter, I wrote Edwin:

> I hate the thought of the South Seas and I have just heard from someone who says it is the most fouled up place imaginable. But that isn't what matters. I feel as though I just don't give a damn anymore. It had looked as though nothing could prevent us having leave together. Edwin, if I write another word about this I will break into tears.[18]

As I readied the letter for mail, events changed again. I handwrote a PS in my letter to Edwin: "Late flash! I may be able to get away from here in about a week. . . . "

After eighteen and one-half months, what was Yakutat? Time passing and some stock-taking, but the future uppermost and the past ever present to whet the appetite for the future.

9   Cape Chiniak

On the day before Christmas 1942, Edwin was transferred from our staging area in Kodiak to a remote outpost, Cape Chiniak. There he would live with five to nine sailors and soldiers until his leave finally came through in mid-June 1944.

It was good for him to be sent to such a place, for it was not dangerous, his deafness would not interfere with his duties, and he would have the opportunity for adventures on his own that were unavailable when we were at Kodiak. But, we would not see each other again until we met up in Washington, D.C., a year and a half later.

Alaska held that romantic charm that satisfied Edwin's lifelong dream to visit. "Isn't it funny," he wrote after being at Cape Chiniak for a few months, "everywhere we go is more beautiful than any place else. When do you suppose it will end?"[1] But Edwin also endured some hardships such as bringing water up on sleds after it froze overnight and lugging in supplies:

> The monthly grub came last week. The truck could only come to within two miles of the station. That means we had to go down and load a cat trailer. After going a half mile, the trailer broke loose and bogged down three feet in the mud. It happened that there was an old sled with great log runners badly worn. We examined it and decided to see what could be done. After transferring the grub from trailer to sled we went on our way and when we got within a half a mile of the station the cat became inextricably stuck in the mire. It was late and there were no trees with which to wench the machine out and all the other army cats were stuck one place or another. We then had to pack all the meat the final half mile, frozen food, too. It was no easy job as the strawberries alone weighed 60 pounds.[2]

There, too, was the garbage, which the cook refused to dispose of, leaving Edwin to do the job:

> I don't mind it at all for the cliff is just a short distance away and distributing all the uneaten bread, etc., to the eagles and gulls is sort

of a rite. I enjoy walking out to the point and slinging the leftovers to the breeze. But, today, while on my way for water, I slipped on the ice. One bucket flew up in the air, came down, and hit me a resounding blow on my derriere, and then went bounding over the cliff fifty feet below, and landed on the rock a sadly battered piece of metal.[3]

Edwin settled into a routine that would give him time for exploring the region and its moss and flora. He loved the area's charm and peacefulness. Sometimes he combed the beach for interesting curiosities, including a sea urchin that would later be used as an ash tray. On occasion, the waves were enormous—forty or fifty feet in height—and spraying eighty feet over the rocks; the wind he described as tempestuous. There, too, was the beautiful little ermine creeping out from under the ice on a snowy day making noises at him and the sea wrack (lumber and seaweed), which he thought looked like a Georgia O'Keefe painting. Edwin also found a sheltered cliffside spot that formed a natural solarium where he could sun himself.

I didn't receive my first letter from Edwin until February 28, although he had posted it weeks earlier. In it he spoke about his cooking experiences, which he described as "wonderful" and the "opportunity to get something edible." Apparently, Eddie, a typical navy cook, would ask Edwin to take over for him whenever he took off for the main base.

I taxed my wits trying to think up something different. Fortunately, the cook left his book—a marvelous twenty-five cent pocket book—but as most of the recipes called for gelatin, whipped cream or some other unheard commodity, I couldn't use them. I did have a braised beef with lots of onions, a wonderful apple pie (not appreciated). . . .[4]

Edwin continued to cook while he was stationed there—and the seamen's appreciation of his culinary talent increased, particularly as one after another "cook" came and left, each worse than the one before. One afternoon, Edwin was rolling out some pastry for an apple pie when

Merrick came strutting in the galley and said, "Well, you'd better get out a big roaster. We are going to have eagle stew for chow tonight." I could have blown up but didn't. Instead I said calmly without even turning, "What are you going to do with it, bury it?" I also asked if he got it on the wing. I might have forgiven him if he hadn't shot it sitting on the cliff. "No," he said, "It was sitting." I was livid. It will be thrown out on the ground like the other two. I am getting sick of running into claws, beaks, and feathers wherever I go. This is the third great bald eagle that has been killed here. Besides being illegal it's such rotten sportsmanship. Silly for me to get worked up over such an issue especially after *Guadalcanal Diary*. I suppose it's just another argument for man's stupidity.[5]

Not all of the men in Edwin's group were so inclined. One of them raised a baby eagle, teaching it to fly, while another cared for a baby fox, just like "a beautiful little puppy."[6]

When Eddie the cook was transferred, his replacement seemed worse, at least from what Edwin relayed to me. "Arkie usually waits until 30 minutes before chow and then runs down and opens a few cans. Such a person! The nearest thing to a dessert he has made was a pot of orange Jello. When I cook, I cook with heart and soul as well as everything else and it exhausts me."[7] Edwin, though, took a fatherly interest in the eighteen-year-old with "U.S.N." tattooed in large letters on his arm.

> He had a finger cut off in a meat grinder and when he was in Seattle the last time contracted a dose of clap. He probably will develop into a nice youngster. I have been working on him. I constantly correct his English but I don't think it makes the slightest impression. He is typical. His mind seems to be preoccupied with sex.[8]

We were both amused and sometimes frustrated by our shipmates. I was drawn to those who seemed to want to make a better future for themselves and who usually expressed opinions about what was going on in the camp or beyond. There were no officers at Edwin's outpost and fewer men stationed there than at mine. But, I was glad to learn that despite obvious differences in background and personalities, "by and large we all get along pretty well as long as we stay out of each other's way. The absence of any strict rules had made it doubly pleasant."[9]

Edwin learned not to wear his intelligence on his sleeve, choosing to "continue being a Pollyanna with those with whom I'll be thrown for God knows how much longer."[10] He said later that the others must see him as a "clam" but "most of the fellows would rather play poker all night than anything else so there you are. It gets mighty boring at times, especially when you hear the same old reminiscences over and over."[11] Edwin, though, did play cribbage until the wee hours of the morning at a cent a hole although it annoyed him to no end when people watched him play.

There were a few men to whom he became somewhat close, such as Merrick, who was in his mid-twenties and engaged to an Italian girl; Arkie, a rural Arkansas teenager whom Edwin found both amusing and troubling; and Nick, the twenty-three-year-old who had dropped out of school to work in a Pennsylvania steel mill before the service. I say "close to" advisedly since Edwin came to feel that "It's a mistake for a small group of people to live together too long when there is no common bond.

Take Merrick and me, for instance. The only thing in common between us is that we are both lousy radio operators."12 Of course, as fellows left, others joined the small melting pot at Chiniak so there was always some new blood.

There was an assortment of people there: Germans, a Hindu, a Croatian, a half-Norwegian/half-Indian, and, of course, a Georgia Cracker, as he sometimes referred to himself. One night, he spent time chatting with Lal, the Hindu, in Hindustani, about the *Gita*, Sarojini Naidu, and Tagore, using phrases from an Indian guidebook. Others at the outpost had a less liberal outlook:

> It annoys me no end when certain ones vent their ire on the British, Negroes, Jews, Eleanor Roosevelt and others. There is nothing much to do about it. My mission is certainly not to reform or to change opinions but I don't hesitate to express myself. Why is it that 100% of Americans are so often intolerant?13

Edwin seemed to be drawn to those in need, like little puppies seeking affection or needing attention. "Isn't it funny," he wondered in one letter, "how I take a fatherly interest in the kids around here?"14 He advised the cook to get his two front teeth fixed and made the appointment for him at the base dentist, saw that he got there, and cooked for him while he was gone. He helped Lal, the Hindu, with his English and tried teaching Nick, the Croat with the engaging smile and pleasing personality, how to type. "He lasted about a week . . . that is more than I expected." But it didn't make any difference to Edwin, who preferred just talking with him since "I do like his frankness and I can be very frank with him, too."15 Edwin helped Nick in other ways:

> Here of late he's been having female trouble and on one occasion he un-bosomed himself to me. I listened patiently for hours and finally advised him not to "call it quits" but to write the girl instead, apologizing for the way he had acted in regard to a letter he had previously written. He never could quite see my point so finally said he would consider doing so if first I wrote the letter for him. He would then make the changes as he saw fit. That was fun. On one of those long watches, I took the time to write about a page—very sweet and apologetic and at the same time firm and a trifle sarcastic. I gave it to him to read and he shook his head. I argued with him and told him he had nothing to lose in sending it. . . . He said he made some slight changes but I wonder. Maybe he disregarded it altogether.16

When Nick departed in February, Edwin wrote him a few letters, but there was never a response. He found Nick "amusing" and was genuinely interested in the well-being of the lad, although the two had little in common.

Toward the end of his stay at Chiniak, however, Edwin met a private at a nearby army unit who stopped by the radio shack for a casual conversation which extended over supper. Learning he was from Macon and had spent some time in Columbus, Edwin asked where he lived in relation to the old Sternberg home in that town. It turned out that was the house he lived in. Their casual conversation turned into a rather lengthy one. The very pleasant private, who was Harvard-educated, had an interest in classical music, especially Tchaikovsky. Well, it seems they listened to Chopin, Grieg, Enesco, Glazounov, and Mozart as well as Tchaikovsky well into the night. A week or so later, Edwin called on the private to take a short hike. Their friendship would be cut short, though, as Edwin was soon transferred to Kodiak.

During his stay at Chiniak, every few months Edwin would journey to the Kodiak base for supplies and a little recreation or a hot shower and steam bath. By hiking five miles he could reach a road along which army trucks passed where he could hitch a ride. On his first trip, he left his camp at 4 P.M. and arrived back at noon the next day. His personal mission was clear:

> The topmost reason of my trip was to acquire an alarm clock. This I was determined to do at any cost. I asked, begged, cajoled, and wheeled everyone I saw. A clerk in the dime store casually said his roommate had two. Such a golden opportunity couldn't be missed, so after a few purchases and a little conversation, I found out when the store closed. . . . Alas, it was too late. What was I to do? Give up? Not little Eddie. As a late customer was coming out of the closed store, I barged in and found out the name of the clerk, address unknown. Then the hunt began. No one knew where Mr. M. C. lived. One person said he was usually in jail. I enquired at hotels, stores, and elsewhere. Finally, a clue was hit upon: "turn left at the bottling works, follow road until you come to Finnish Baths and inquire there." That settled that. Mr. C. had an apartment above the baths and when I walked in he greeted me somewhat embarrassedly. I fell at his roommate's knees and implored him to part with one of his clocks. He seemed pleased to be of patriotic service and forthwith handed over the object. It now awakens me each morning and allows me to enjoy calm and peaceful sleep.[17]

Edwin loved his morning watch where he was alone in the radio shack with no interruptions. "I only have to check the equipment periodically, usually every hour and this just takes a few minutes. After that I can read or write until the minute hand completes another revolution of the clock."[18] Edwin could peer through a window in his shack to the sea beyond. He said it reminded him of some shots in the spooky film *Ladies in Retirement*.

When not on watch, he often sat at a small Sheraton desk where he wrote letters (including some for his mates) or reclined in a big leather lounge chair to enjoy reading a letter he'd received. Edwin once wrote of receiving fifty pieces of mail at one time. Nevertheless, sometimes folks did not respond to letters as promptly as he liked. Carson's cousin, Topie, did not write for a couple of months, leaving Edwin to wonder if him asking whether she had seen a partridge pea, a leguminous plant that grows in the South, was what had caused the delay.

Letters were of the greatest importance in keeping our spirits high, and the answering of them consumed many hours that might otherwise have been spent boringly. Edwin received mail from many of the same folks as I did—my aunts, my mother, my sisters—and I received letters and gifts from his family. We were like one big family, interrelated and loving. We sometimes shared these letters or anecdotes (once Edwin told me of an advertisement in the Columbus Ledger: "For Sale: a partially trained skunk"). Or sometimes we just divided the goodies like candy and nuts that had been sent along. We discussed family news, exchanged photographs, and swapped amusing anecdotes from our friends. For instance, Minor, I learned, had been kicked out of the Santa Fe USO because he advocated giving free beer and cigarettes to the soldiers. So he formed his own USO. We chatted about movies which we had seen or classical music we had listened to from records or on a radio broadcast. Sometimes we passed along books or magazines.

But we corresponded differently to those who corresponded to each of us. George Scheirer was generous to a fault, not only in writing to each of us regularly but also in sending magazines, books, records—and even 100 dollars each for a furlough fund. I was inclined to write more carefully to George, with an emphasis on what I was reading. Edwin's letters usually had something humorous in them. From George's point of view, he seemed to enjoy our letters and really felt needed:

> I'm sorry that you and John had to part—all the more would I like to be a connecting link between you both, even though I realize that, like any other triangle, the sum of two sides is greater and how very much I know well than the third. Even so, I would be the third side.[19]

In the fall of 1943, Edwin chipped in with Merrick, whom he said had "a musical IQ of 2," to buy a portable electric record player from a serviceman returning to the States.[20] Although the player was fine, the records that accompanied it were

> not so good, a few popular things, Dinah Shore, Harry James, and a dismal hymn, "In the Garden" as interpreted by the Hour of Charm All Girl Personality Orchestra and Choir with Vivian and her magic violin. So far, no Sinatra but he's bound to pop up any day. We have

a variety of musical tastes at our station. I prefer long hair, the soldiers and other radiomen like Jive and our eighteen-year-old cook from Arkansas dotes on "git-tar music" and hymns. Said cook is a scream. His favorite number is a hillbilly ballad called "The Great Speckled Bird." I have been gunning with him. The last time I had good fun singing "The Wabash Cannonball," another one of his loves.[21]

Sometimes he would fill me in on his friend Carson, whom I had yet to meet. She "has a date with Reeves after the war on the terrace at the Brevoort and has promised him six stingers. Invited me to join them."[22] Later, he wrote: "I don't think Carson and Reeves will ever go back together. She thinks he should marry an 'uncomplicated woman,' have a home, settle down and have children, and for herself she will face life alone."[23] When I did meet Carson after the war, she became a dear friend and often spent time with us in Charleston.

Like many servicemen, mail was important to us, but, unlike most, our companionship would have been frowned upon by the authorities. Although Edwin and I each met a few other homosexuals in the service, neither of us knew anyone in our situation. As lovers before the war, we sometimes reminisced about our life before the war. This was done carefully and in somewhat coded language, as when Edwin remembered our anniversary: "I can't realize it's been three years since the summer on the Isle of Palms."[24] Letters were always read by a censor and subject to the censor's knife. "Was it you," Edwin asked, who said "one of my letters looked like a paper doll?"[25]

But, by virtue of having similar military assignments, we also shared a life together during the war, albeit one separated by glaciers and mountain ranges—and the interminable delay of the mail.

> I suppose you have been expecting a letter from me for some time. For two weeks all of our little crew has been on edge in anticipation of the monthly mail. It's that way every month now (except it seems to be getting worse) for two weeks after the mail arrives all is well. We are kept fairly busy answering letters, ruminating over certain passages, events, and what not. Then come the two muggy weeks of waiting for another sack. That you are living the life of a monk doesn't sound so good. You know there are all sorts of tales about monks.[26]

With springtime, Edwin seemed to enjoy the outdoors even more. He began to do a little painting and carvings out of whalebones as well as starting a Victory Garden with four rows of about ten feet each of carrots, muskmelon, spinach, and kale. He also kept a journal about all of the native plants he found, preferring to "go alone because I like to dilly-dally.

... I try not to miss a thing. My list is approaching 50 blooming plants."[27] In his letters, he often relayed detailed information about the plants he spotted or stories of his escapades in the woods.

> Isn't it strange how differently things impress people? I have in mind a certain bird. You probably know it, at least its distinctive call. I had been thinking what a sweet, gentle call it has, a beautiful love song. In fact, I mentioned the numerous songbirds to Merrick. He said there was one, and then he initiated the call, that sounded so disgusted it almost drove him nuts. So there you have it. I am disillusioned. I have just decided he (the bird) is singing "Don't Get Around Much Anymore." The first three notes are identical.[28]

He associated other birds with popular songs, such as the Alaska Hermit Thrush with "Three Blind Mice."

Throughout the spring and into the summer, Edwin feared that he might be transferred. But, by midsummer, he had found out that

> it looks as though I'm a fixture here for some time yet with no change in rate in sight but I'm satisfied. The bleak hills in plain sight from our window are an indication of a far less attractive station to which I might be sent. The better rate would just saddle me with responsibilities with which I couldn't possibly cope without months of practical experience.[29]

Edwin liked the farmhouse idea, particularly my sketches of it. Like me, he felt he had wasted years doing office work. But, as time at Cape Chiniak elapsed, he became a bit more skeptical, taking a "wait and see" attitude. He thought I should "spend the first six months or a year after the war finishing your novel."[30] Edwin was always supportive of my writing ambition and often encouraged me after reading a verse or short story I would send him. He was particularly enthusiastic about "Day Off," writing: "it's one of the best things you've done.... I predict a war bond to well your till."[31] When I wrote with grand news that I had won, Edwin was in "a concert pitch, whatever that means." He "resurrected" my short story just before going to bed: "This second reading—six months later—reveals many hidden beauties. The mood you capture intrigues me. While reading it, I find myself in that same mood. After reading the story I dropped off to sleep and had pleasant dreams."[32]

Edwin had been less supportive of the farm idea, but the concept of a farm inn was somewhat more appealing. He saw his frequent baking at the camp as an opportunity to learn to cook for a group and as a way to improve his considerable culinary skills if we opened it.

Similarly, when I had broached the prospect of us sharing a romantic leave together, he was more realistic. "I don't see how we could possibly get off at the same time. Maybe I'll feel differently by next winter...."³³ A month later, he seemed ambivalent, "hardly know what to do. Unless it is urgent, I don't suppose I'll take any leave."³⁴ He continued to express ambivalence as each month passed, citing concerns about the expense, duration, and effort for a transcontinental trip, the weather, or my lack of practicality.

At midsummer, Edwin went on his longest hike, joined by two of his mates. He had wanted to climb the towering mountain since his arrival. After spending all night on watch, he cajoled two of his mates into going on what he billed as "a mountain climb and bear hunt, a veritable safari. ... It was tough going through the thickets of berry bushes, willows, and ferns. The fine view from the summit was a reward for our efforts. No bears were encountered but many tracks and trails and other evidence were noted."³⁵

In late September, a letter came explaining one of several accidents that Edwin had while in Alaska:

> For a week I have been drifting in sort of a void.... While scurrying down Merrick's rustic walk, which happened to be wet, I slipped and was catapulted forward in an inverted position and all the weight of my body sent my forehead toward a spruce crosspiece. It happened with such swiftness I wasn't aware of what was taking place, but as soon as I raised my hand to my head I knew. There was a knot the size of an egg that threatened to grow larger.³⁶

A few days later, Edwin was back out hiking to enjoy

> the brilliant fall colors and the scenery along the way.... In the woods the deciduous foliage is yellowing and the berries of elder and Hercules Club are a glistening red. Vast patches of Kodiak grass, lately a lush green, is now seen. Those mountains bare of trees except scrubby vegetation are now various shades of yellow, brown, red, purple. The higher ranges are streaked with white as a result of activity in the upper atmosphere.³⁷

In early October, Edwin returned from Kodiak where he had gone with Merrick and another serviceman "in a wretched state." It seems

> as the bank was closed, I couldn't get any money. The dentist was full up.... The Igloo's Christmas cards were something to gasp at and run to the nearest bar, which was exactly what I did. There, I struck up with my cronies and amid wild confusion we started out systematic drinking. To me the Kodiak beers are infinitely more lethal than the Kodiak bears.³⁸

Figure 9.1 Edwin at Camp Chiniak, Alaska.

Edwin then "went reeling" down to Erskine's general store where

> Immediately I pounced on an organ recording of the Bach C-Minor Passacaglia. It would not have taken any keen salesmanship to sell me the album but *una voce poco* said, "No" and instead I sought out the clerk and plied her with questions about "The Great Speckled Bird" and "The Wabash Cannonball." My efforts to making a purchase

were abortive so amused she was at my speech difficulties. The clerk, one of the nicest persons I've met (or rather seen) in ages put me at liberty to go through all the records. Being in such a wobbly state, I took leave of her, promising to return. . . . Back to the bar there remained thirty minutes to kill before the serious drinking began, so I ambled down to the Finnish baths. . . . Merrick had come up and told me he was staying over and by some curious prestidigitation I later found myself wandering around with a stack of records—the last thing in the world I should have been trusted with. At long last, we got started and somewhere between Kodiak and G. a scuffling drunk slid onto the bench beside me and the first thing I knew the records had disappeared. The entire stack had been pushed onto the road. In my partial dim-out I couldn't quite gather what had taken place but it didn't take me long to come to. I was livid. There was nothing to do then so I didn't cry. The return trip was torture of a sort but also amusing, as when another drunk lay down and put his head in my lap and went to sleep. . . . I wonder what Merrick will say when he finds out the fate of his records?[39]

Edwin enjoyed not only classical music but also spirituals, especially those sung by the contralto Marian Anderson as well as popular tunes which he sometimes sang to himself, one of which he shared with me, "You'd be so nice to come home to."

Edwin read less than I (usually only when he was on a watch), and his reading interest was somewhat different. "I find Proust increasingly difficult now. P. G. Wodehouse is more to my taste."[40] He really enjoyed the Australian writer Xavier Herbert's 649-page *Capricornia* but "before I've read another long book it will be snowing again; before I've finished Proust the war will probably be over."[41]

Of course, I exercised much less than Edwin. Later that October, he told me an amusing story of one of his all-day hikes, which he took religiously when he had time off.

I took our new striker out to show him the country. I had been to this cove before and I knew just how far it was and how tough. So, I warned him. Being from Utah and ten years my junior (it seems I'm ten or twenty years older than everybody in the Navy), I gathered that he was quite an alpinist and wouldn't have the least bit of trouble keeping up with a cracker from the Georgia flatlands. I was wrong.

From the beginning, Johnson was always far in the rear and by the time we reached our destination his leg muscles were aching. I left him to build a fire to boil water for tea and took off my shoes and socks in order to cross a wide icy stream to a grassy meadow where some logs had drifted. . . . I made my way through the icy water again and in doing so soaked my trousers. Imagine my annoyance to find that no fire had been made, nor wood gathered, and we only had about twenty minutes before beginning the trek back to the station.

Johnson had given me his knife so he couldn't cut kindling. . . . So I took off the wet trousers and went down on the beach to gather wood while Johnson whittled a few chips. The fire was duly started but as the damned thing never generated more than two calories of heat, we had to do without the hot tea and instead wash our sandwiches down with ice water.

At the appointed time, I put on my wet pants and we began the return trip. It was just as well that the dungarees didn't dry for a misty rain blew in from the sea and in no time at all we both looked like wet weasels. Johnson's legs began to ache and we had about seven miles (in a straight line) to go over extremely tough terrain, pushing through spiny salmonberry canes, sticky spruce needles, and slippery willows, down two ravines a hundred feet deep and almost straight up on the other side. It seemed that I was always a quarter of a mile ahead of Johnson. This was fortunate for I couldn't have borne his suffering . . . with the determination of a Swede he plodded on though he was hardly able to lift his legs. Later he said he had aged fifty years. . . . At 1705 we reached the station and Johnson had to go on watch at 1700. . . . I felt all right and except for a small blister on my heel, I wouldn't have known I had been out.[42]

In November, Edwin wrote that he had made Radioman Second Class. He began about this time to speak of leave and what options it would bring. Throughout the month, he was having second thoughts, preferring just to sit back and wait and pointing out the couple of hundred ahead of him on the list. But, in the same letter, he reported that the cook, who had only put in for leave a week before, was ordered to report to base. It was such vagaries in how the military operated that perplexed Edwin and maddened me.

He suggested that we always use Mrs. Schwab's apartment house in San Francisco for mail drop-offs if we found ourselves there. As it turned out, that is just where we would meet almost two years later. He also marveled at how our letters were duplicates in some respects. "Yours of Sept. 16 tells of crazy flashes in your mind about certain past events. Just about that time I was writing you some similar observations. . . . I have thought of Milagra and the little Cuban boys diving for pennies in Key West."[43]

Before Christmas, I learned from Edwin that running water was finally being installed in the galley, though he still had to go to the army base for showers. His locker was jammed more each day with the many gifts he received—including mine. "The cook said I was acting like a little kid about those presents. That coming from an eighteen-year-old! Why at his age I was still hanging up my stocking."[44]

This was our second Christmas apart, but he seemed to have enjoyed himself as he helped prepare the turkey dinner, writing later: "I haven't yet told you how much I appreciate your remembering me in so many nice ways."⁴⁵ He added a humorous comment:

> I like your morbid letters equally as well as your gay ones. Guess what I was thinking of yesterday? Remember the time I jumped out the 1050 Post Street and said 'boo' to a strange woman (thinking it was you)? That was the nadir of mad doings in San Francisco!

In mid-March, Edwin was moved from Cape Chiniak to the base at Kodiak, where he would stay the last two months of his tour in Alaska. "The transition is not particularly hard to take, only it is so dull and stupid having to sit by the hour with those old phones draped over one's head." Since Edwin was rusty on code, he was tutored by an experienced radioman to get up to speed and to learn more code. This time "in a semi-state of regimentation," contrasted sharply to fifteen months with "a room of one's own for hours without interruption (except to step to the door to take a leak or view the aurora borealis or listen to the ocean's roar) was such an ideal arrangement that it seems unbelievable now."⁴⁶ After eleven days there he wrote telling me it "seems more like years than days. . . ."⁴⁷ As the days passed into weeks he became more adamant about not returning to Alaska when he was reassigned after taking leave in June.

In mid-April, Edwin had his first experience of skiing, which he shared with me:

> I just called the chalet and was told the snow was pretty nice. . . . My day in the mountains was wonderful and as a result I look as though I'd spent a summer in New Mexico. I had a multitude of spills and once my arm got badly snapped, nothing worse than that. My God! I didn't know the human anatomy could possibly get in so many positions. One moment I was on my head and in another I was on my tail—mostly the latter. You should have seen my long legs all tangled up with skis and poles. It is a great sport, but it's plenty of work.⁴⁸

May was a time of waiting, frustrations, letters back and forth about plans for leave. Edwin felt in limbo at Kodiak, restless when not on watches, lacking the outdoor pleasures of Cape Chiniak which were such a joy to him. He found it hard to write letters, to read, to concentrate. It wasn't as bad for me as I had more duties and less time to myself. I was writing to Edwin almost every day. The last letter that came from Edwin in Alaska was written June 7. "I'm pretty much p. o. at the delay in getting away but know how it is. Worse still, I'm afraid there'll be a longer delay in Bremerton than I expected. So you might as well settle down with Krafft-Ebing or the Bible for a few more weeks."[49] I chose the former.

This was the last letter I was ever able to keep from Edwin while we were in the service. On June 27, I left by train for Bremerton heading to South Carolina.

10 Reunion

I arrived at the Charleston train station on the evening of July 2, 1944 after a lengthy transcontinental trip. The next morning, as I sat in my room on the top floor of 9 College Street to write Edwin, there was a gentle breeze with an overcast sky. "I have been looking at books and going through things, searching for a few things out of our wonderful past."[1] Outside the front window, the sycamore was beautiful, and the college was quiet and full of its own beauty. "This attic room speaks of you in so many ways and while nothing could make me long for you more than I have, it makes me want you differently somehow." Our relationship, though, like the neighborhood, seemed unchanged by war.

The next day, I wrote from the family place on Ocean Drive after receiving a letter that said Edwin would not be able to get away for a while. "I just couldn't sleep last night for thinking of seeing you after all. Then, today, your letter from Seattle came and with it all hope flew out of the window for the dozenth time. . . . What has happened to our luck?"[2]

In spite of my pleasure at being with the family, I was depressed and tired, but I tried to appear relaxed and spent hours regaling the family with navy stories. I began swimming, ate voraciously, reclined on the porch, listened, and talked. Everyone was in good health, happy, and spoiling me. I ended my letter to Edwin on that July Fourth (marking our fourth-year anniversary) saying, "We must keep close to each other in our letters, for it seems there is no other way. I will write often. I have so much to tell you but all I want to tell you is that I love you and always shall."[3]

I heard from Edwin a couple of times and learned that he might be able to leave shortly. More plans were made. "I would love to be with you alone somewhere for a few days," I wrote, as I no longer signed my letters "your cousin" but "all my love."[4]

Meanwhile, George's letter arrived in Charleston. He, too, was anxious to see Edwin and me.

> It is hard to write when one's mind is occupied only with the D-Day of your invasion of Alban Towers. May it come soon. I cannot be

liberated soon enough.... How I long for the day when Edwin and John and George can walk through a nice woods. Edwin will scamper about after birds' nests and (I hope) keep the snakes interested elsewhere; and John will peer at various flora with a magnifying glass; and George . . . ? He, as I told Edwin, will utter hoarse cries indicative of lunch time or resting time—in fact, of any excuse to halt and lie around and talk. Or even not talk; just to be near together would mean so much.[5]

I was going to leave Charleston on the 16th for Washington, where I would stay with George for nine days. I needed to return to Bremerton for reassignment, which would not be Alaska.

Luck finally caught up again with us. When I heard from Edwin that he would arrive in Washington at George Scheirer's on July 19, I immediately left by bus to join him. Edwin and I arrived in Washington almost at the same time! We had the bedroom of George's sister, who moved in with a neighbor. We would stretch out on the floor and listen to music; sometimes Edwin would cook.

Edwin had never met George, though they had corresponded since he was stationed at Cape Chiniak. Of course, Edwin was enchanted with him. When Edwin was in the last couple of months in Alaska, after two years of correspondence with him, George wrote:

John Donne seems to have been interested equally in the preservation of his soul and the pleasures of the bed. However, a little of each goes a long way.... If two people differ on this or that point, what is that compared with the fondness and affection in which they hold one another? ... We have chosen our friends for certain definite characteristics that we love and react to, and great is the sorrow at their loss. Equally great is the joy at their impending furloughs.[6]

George seemed euphoric about Edwin's pending return. "Well, Edwin, how I wish you were here now! Come as quickly as you can."[7]

My reunion with Edwin was everything that I had hoped for, with various social gatherings among old friends who seemed eager to entertain us. George's beautiful apartment was a refuge from the many social engagements with friends from my "Jeb and Dash" days. Nell Bass invited many friends to one big party. Edward Newbury and Bob Aldredge had another party, with about ten persons attending, including Phil Bell, Bo, Perks, and Carter. In his diary of July 20, Carter ("Jeb") wrote:

A delight to see good old John again after four years and months. Except for thinning hair he didn't seem to have changed any. He had with him his friend Edwin Peacock.... Had an extremely pleasant evening.... all old friends of John and probably chosen by him for

Figure 10.1 George Scheirer and John in Washington, D.C.

invitation. I had perhaps five or six highballs during the evening. We had a good time in conversation, joking and badinage, and recalling old times. . . . Edwin seems a fine, friendly, sweet-natured chap—a very good looking youth with dark, curly hair. He told me he knew me already because he had heard so much about me from John. I wish I could see both of them again but they are only here through Sunday and have many people to see and things to do. It was almost two when the party broke up. At the sidewalk I said goodbye again to John and Edwin and came in. I wish both of them the best of luck from the depths of my heart.[8]

The time rushed by too quickly, with little time for the beauties of Washington, although we did some sightseeing. Nell took us out in her car one afternoon when we had a little spare time. We had dinner out each evening and went to places that charged high prices but failed to live up to their reputation. The best meals were those Bob's mother prepared over the weekend. We had a good time with Edward, hiking in the Maryland countryside and listening to records. Being with George, of course, was best of all since he was not with us when we were with our other friends. There was still not enough time for all the things that were stored away in the brain to be said to Edwin.

At week's end, I said goodbye to Edwin and George at the train station. Edwin left soon afterward for Thomasville, Georgia. Afterward, George wrote him: "A week can be so long and so short. But the comforting feeling to me is that you left with me a good part of yourself and so I cannot say that you have really gone away. In trying to squeeze many years into such a short time, I grew fonder of you each day."[9]

I took the train for Bremerton, with an overnight stop in Chicago, where from the LaSalle Hotel, I wrote Edwin without the need to worry about navy censors:

> To have been with you under such happy circumstances made up for the many disappointments of the past few months. It was good to find you unchanged in your affection as in your own sweet nature. Now I can gird my loins for the next year and a half or whatever it will be. It will be much easier to bear since I have seen you. When I got on the train for Chicago, I was compensated in my misery by the thought that you would be with me again some day—and that seems enough to ask for.[10]

While in Chicago, I made the most of my time, seeing *Between Two Worlds*, visiting the art museum, and going to the service center to listen to some records. I later wrote Edwin about the late evening's adventure.

> I was stopped by a kid who wanted to take me to a cathouse (did I look so lonely or hard up?) and later wandered alone into a

downtown bar, the Town Casino. It was not very full, but was evidently patronized by some gay people. I talked with a very nice fellow sitting next to me and he suggested we try some other place. We finally got to a bar—the Capitol Lounge—where there was a good Dixieland band and we drank and talked for several hours. You would have been amused by the conversation. I talked about you and he talked about his friend, George, who has been away in S.A. for two years. This fellow teaches English at a military school.[11]

On the train the next day, my seatmate was a middle-aged priest, who taught at a Midwestern college. He invited me to have a drink in the club car and then for dinner, which I enjoyed. After the meal, he went back to the club car, and I excused myself as I wanted to get to bed. The berths were made up, mine the lower one. I took off my jumper and was sitting with my legs outside of the curtain to take off my shoes when the priest returned. He asked me if he could sit on the bunk with me for a while and said that I could continue undressing. I took off my pants and, with the curtain closed, he asked me what the boys in Yakutat did for sex. I said I didn't know. He hesitated then said, "Did they ever, er, er, sixty-nine?" I said not to my knowledge. He leaned over, kissed me on the cheek, and said, "You're a good boy, John" and went to his upper berth. The next day he avoided me.

I arrived in Bremerton on August 1st and was immediately put on a radio circuit, where I did very badly. On the 12th I learned that I was to go to school to prepare for transfer to an attack transport, the U.S.S. *Dickens*. The crew of the *Dickens* was stationed in a barracks where we became acquainted as we awaited a cruise on a similar ship.

In late July, George wrote "with what restraint this letter will be written only you and I can know." He continued

> You will understand because that brown-eye glance of yours discovered much. And I have no words beautiful enough to express that feeling which, like the anguished silent prayers, comes from the core of being and is all-enveloping. To see and take hold of you after all these years have brought to reality all the pictures missing from our letters—letters which, in some ways, must be unique. They were honest letters and they always will be. Your visit is the deep blue sea after a long journey over the arid desert in which letters were the oases for life-giving refreshment. And so I feel refreshed and can only hope that you do, too.[12]

Upon leaving Washington, Edwin went first to Charleston and on to Thomasville, where his family showered on him the affection they would always feel. Later he visited his cousin and her family at Fort Myers before starting out on August 9 for the Small Craft Training Center, Terminal

Island, California. He began duties at the Center at San Pedro five days later. However, on September 16, he was transferred to the radio shack of the Naval Receiving Barracks in Portland.

My "practice" ship stayed within the Sound and, in October, anchored at Astoria while we awaited the commissioning of the *Dickens*. That allowed me the good fortune of having weekend liberty twice in Portland, where I met up with Edwin. We found a hotel, ate well, explored the city, and went to a concert by the Metropolitan Opera soprano Grace Moore, a glamorous singer who was in good voice. This would be the last time we were together for nearly a year.

After the *Dickens* was commissioned we stayed in the waters around Astoria for two weeks. There were seventy-six men in our small compartment, and I was sleeping on the third tier of bunks. By getting up just before 5:30 A.M., I could dress before the narrow aisles became crowded. I was put on radio watch in charge of two other radiomen. When we finally left Astoria via Puget Sound and reached the wide mouth of the Columbia River and went into the Pacific, the seas were cavernous, and the *Dickens* tossed, sending tables crashing to the floor, objects hurtling through the air, and sailors dashing to the rails. By eleven I succumbed, but when we reached calmer waters, I was all right. That was to be my first of many bouts with seasickness.

11 Edwin's Discharge

Edwin had been miserable at San Pedro and was happy to be sent to Portland on September 18, where he went aboard a degaussing ship. He thought his hearing problem would get him out of radio, but it didn't.

I was happy also that Edwin was transferred given that I was still at a nearby port. "I am excited as a child or as myself can be at such time," I wrote George. "I feel as though whatever is in me can't be contained in this poor body. Well, you know our secret, which we never wanted to be a secret from you, and so you must forgive my rantings."[1]

On my visit of August 26 to Edwin, we first discussed the idea of having a bookshop in Charleston on the ground-floor basement at 9 College Street. We were enthusiastic about this, and I wrote my Aunt Peggy to get her opinion. At that time, Edwin was working in his off hours as a tree surgeon. He was climbing telephone poles with straps and ropes, cutting limbs from around live wires. He resigned after two days.

Meanwhile, Edwin and George continued to correspond, as I did. "Soon I suppose you will be seeing, John," George said. A bit annoyed that he had not heard from Edwin since his last letter, he continued with a quotation from Romain Rolland, who "has written about Jean-Christophe, may I not have a friend called John-Edwin who means everything to me and from whom it is only natural for me to hope for response in kind?"[2] After hearing from both Edwin and me, George beamed: "What could I do now without you two friends! . . . I have read and re-read your letter and John's and now I know that the love of John-Edwin justifies existence. . . . Now I know there is happiness. . . . "[3]

Edwin found Portland delightful. He loved the parks, beautiful with roses, and met some interesting people. One of them was a fireman who had written and taken the photographs for a beautiful book on the ghost towns of the West. He and Edwin became intimate—Edwin keeping me informed of the progress of their "affair," knowing that I would not be jealous.

Edwin had a calmness here that he hadn't had since leaving Cape Chiniak. To supplement his income, he took on a part-time job in a canning factory, where he lifted heavy boxes. Edwin had to quit this job when he strained himself badly. He then went to work in a saw mill, shoveling sawdust on conveyer belts. For this he received thirty dollars for four evenings, from 5 P.M. until 1:30 in the morning.

Before his change of job, I wrote George that

> I don't care to have him lifting hundred pound bags of stuff. There is a record of too many heart ailments among the men of his family and even when getting into the Navy, he had to have several examinations.... He is rather sensitive about this, so we don't mention it. He is always inclined to overdo.[4]

In late December, Edwin left Portland for Monterey, where he would be assigned to the yacht that had once belonged to the actor Joel McCrea.[5] This boat would patrol the waters of the area. It went aground one night. Edwin was aroused from his bunk and joined the other sailors in jumping overboard, where they landed in water up to their knees.

Early in 1945, his commanding officer finally recognized that Edwin had a serious hearing problem. In December, Edwin had put in a request with the view toward a change in his rating because of "irremediable physical disability." He was no longer able to hear many of the commands, signals, and verbal orders on board the ship to which he had been assigned a month earlier. In endorsing Edwin's request, his commanding officer wrote: "Peacock is considered by all officers aboard to be one of the ablest, most willing, and conscientious of any petty officers of their knowledge."[6] He recommended a higher rating and shore duty.

During this time, Edwin often went to Laguna Beach, striking up acquaintance with a group of gay men not in the service.[7] He enjoyed having people to talk with frankly and told them about "John." He was more relaxed and happy than he had been since leaving Portland. I wrote Edwin, "Never disparage what gives your old cousin so much pleasure. Those little trips to Laguna Beach sound like fun."[8]

He had hearing tests throughout February and March in Long Beach. I was delighted to hear that these tests showed a slight improvement. Writing to Edwin, I asked: "Do you attribute that to the scarcity of liquor in Alaska and the giving up of cigarettes?"[9] I added, "I cannot feel too bad about your being at the hospital still, for they might send you to a thousand worse places. Have you thought of what you would do if you got out?" George, also responding to Edwin's letters, quipped: "Your hospital sounds like Radio City. Is there a statue of Promiscuous in front of the prophylaxis station? ... Naval examinations must, like the Army, be conducted with an end in view."[10] In another, responding to Edwin's annoyance about being so long interred for evaluation—or in his words, "a cross between a god and a jackass"—George tried to lighten Edwin's mood telling him about seeing in the "dim recesses" of a hotel men's-only bar "an Army officer and a Navy officer [who] sat holding hands and one

84   *War Years*

constantly intercepted burning glances. Really, I should get out more and observe wartime Washington in its more intimate ass-pects."[11]

Stationed at Long Beach, Edwin was given light duties. One of his hospital duties was to assist in painting the outside of a tall building. He said that the rickety scaffolding made mountain climbing seem tame. I also learned that he had more time off:

> I like to hear of your frolicking. It reminds me that life is not all radio and steel decks. I do not have to be reminded of your friendship, that star to this wandering bark within a bark. I think there is an earlier letter I have not received as you mention Philadelphia in terms that imply you may be going there.[12]

He was transferred to the Naval Hospital in Philadelphia and was allowed weekend leave. He had a weekend visit with George in Washington, later remarking on the "lonesome souls" he encountered wandering Dupont Circle.[13] I later received a letter from George saying that

> he is very well and looks tall, lean, tanned, and healthy as ever. We talked until 1:30 in the morning and quaffed manhattans until Edwin began talking about "boondoggling" and then inquired, "Just what am I talking about?" At that point we retired. . . . Early this morning, I mentioned standing on one's head, whereupon Edwin got out of bed and demonstrated the result of considerable recent practice—a new way, by having a three point contact with the floor, head, and both elbows. It was a perfect and superb rising up of his column of strength. . . . Edwin is greatly taken with the California sunshine and climate and wants to go back to San Francisco and do defense work when he is discharged.[14]

George wrote enthusiastically about a visit to see Edwin in Philadelphia. This was the first time he had been out of Washington since 1937. They had dinner at Bookbinders Restaurant, famous for its fish dinners and old photographs and theater programs of England and early America. Praising Edwin's qualities as a host, George relayed: "He is doing well and expects a discharge but hardly dares to count on it. I tried talking when he wasn't looking and he didn't hear me. . . . He is required to take a two month course in lip reading."[15]

In late April, Edwin visited Carson at Nyack, N.Y., where her mother had bought a house that would become McCullers' permanent home after the death of Reeves. She and Reeves had remarried. When I learned of that from Edwin, I wrote back. "Didn't I tell you so? I think they belong together, like Georgia and South Carolina or music and poetry."[16] I turned out to be quite wrong.

One evening Edwin went to Baltimore to see an old friend. He missed the fellow and was wandering aimlessly when he heard his name called. It was Edward Newbury, who was there with his lover Bob, his sister Betty, and his mother to see a play. They talked until time for the performance. Bob had just received a medical discharge because of a nervous breakdown; Edward had been excused from military service because he had vision in only one eye. They went back to Charlotte to continue civilian lives as banker and architect.

Edwin was fitted with his first hearing aid and received his honorable discharge on June 1. He went to see George, who wrote:

> I'm staying in this morning while E. is downtown choosing a new suit. He seems undecided and I shouldn't be surprised if he were to come back empty-handed. He is wearing his "whites" now. . . . P.S. Edwin was here when I came back from having a bite of lunch and, as the Arabs say, he was looking like the full moon in the fourteenth day, i.e., a cross between Ronald Colman (as he said to tell you) and a S.O.B. Anyway, he is a splendid sight in powder blue tropical worsted. . . . [17]

From Washington, Edwin stopped in Charleston to see my relatives before going on to Thomasville. At home, he worked hard, canning, gardening, repairing, and even tending to the cemetery lot with fresh leaf mold and pruning shears. At Fort Myers, later, he gathered dozens of shells on nearby Captiva Island to send to George, removing his shorts while doing so. The sun smote him fiercely on his fanny, and he had to sleep on his front for several nights.

After a couple of months, Edwin was bored with his "unproductive" life and started out for Tulsa and Santa Fe on August 1. But the lure of San Francisco was too great, and he soon found himself there, working in an Oreo factory. He occasionally met with several of the people we had known when working in the Finance Office. He expected me to show up in San Francisco and wanted to be there when I arrived.

12 At Sea

> I saw the city like a crumbling tomb
> Laid starkly open to the dusty sky:
> Her river scarcely moved, so still in gloom
> She seemed, with only ghostly traffic standing by.
> A broken length of walls, a spire, a dome,
> Wrote their historic lines across the morning:
> Here desolation found her newest home
> And waste made eloquent her latest warning.
> I thought a moment death must be like this
> An empty city of gray silent spaces,
> Until I walked the streets and saw the kiss
> Of life brave people give to ruined places,
> The Filipinos building with their will
> A brighter jewel than their shattered pearl.
> Spring in Manila

We began our shakedown (or perhaps it should have been called "shake up") cruise almost at once. When we seemed prepared to travel the great Pacific, we headed for San Francisco.

We anchored in the Bay near the Oakland Bridge, the sun shining brightly and a cool wind blowing. It was a Friday afternoon, and I asked the Executive Officer if I could be taken ashore to hear the San Francisco Symphony Orchestra. He was so astonished that a radioman wanted to hear a symphony that he arranged for a boat. During intermission, the eightyish little lady sitting next to me turned and asked me in a quivering voice where I had been. "A place you've never heard of," I said. "Yakutat, Alaska." She replied, "Indeed I've heard of Yakutat. Fifty years ago I hunted bear there for the Smithsonian Institution."

After going to have one of Mrs. Helwig's chicken pot pies at her little restaurant, I didn't want to return right away to the ship. Why not go to the baths, I thought. It would be a long time before I would have an opportunity for sex. This time I didn't quiver at the door. I sat for a while in the towel-clad lounge, enjoyed the steam room, and thought that a bath like this one is the most honest of democracies. Bankers and barbers, policemen and poetasters are anonymous, and each bather can usually find someone who shares his fantasies. I didn't have any fantasies but was happy to find that there was someone for me, too. As William Blake said, "The road of excess leads to the palace of wisdom."[1]

After a couple of days, we went to Long Beach where we had overnight liberty. I took public transportation to Hollywood and the famous Hollywood Canteen, where starlets and stars came to dance with or entertain enlisted men. That night, the legendary Sophie Tucker sang to great applause. Everyone was friendly, and one young black man was particularly so with me. He had acted with Tallulah Bankhead on Broadway and had come to Hollywood to try his luck, which had been bad thus far.

I relayed one of those stories to George:

> He is a friend of her maid's and accepted a job one evening at her house (thinking Bankhead had forgotten him) to help serve dinner. When Tallulah saw him she threw her arms around him and kissed him in front of the guests. "My God, what are you doing in my house? This is my very old friend everybody."[2]

Of course, given the military censors, I didn't dare write George that this actor asked me to go back to his apartment with him. I was delighted and stayed with him until daylight, when I had to return to the ship. There would be no more such adventures while I was in the Navy.

On December 5th, we headed for Hawaii, where we remained about two weeks. I was sent ashore to procure classical and popular records for the ship from naval stores and had other occasions to be ashore when I could enjoy the Royal Hawaiian Hotel's swimming pool, recently taken over by the Navy. I took an island tour and saw the vast pineapple fields and the ordinary tourist sites, including a performance of the hula. There were rainbows almost every day, and, on one occasion, we passed under the end of a rainbow. Alas, there was no pot of gold there.

On Christmas Day, I was feeling pensive, overlooking the rail, watching the flying fish as their movements rippled the water. I seemed to be living in the center of an onboard stillness that was of my own making. For some months, I had been despondent. I had been violently ill for many weeks, often having to summon a radioman to take over my position. But none of the physical pain, the nausea, had been as hard to bear as the malaise of spirit that had come over me. I spent sleepless nights, the sweat pouring from my body in the humid, crowded compartment with its sleeping cries, musty odors, and startling movements of my youthful shipmates, who called me "Uncle John" and looked upon my idiosyncrasies as the manifestations of encroaching senility at the ripe age of thirty-two. Often I felt I could not go on living, and I looked into the blue waters of the Pacific for long, weary hours when I was not on duty. There were moments when a word or gesture could have sent me to eternal sleep. Thoughts of Edwin, however, kept me sane. Writing Edwin about my "disease of darkness," George observed:

> John means everything that is good, and light, and clear. Even were he in a melancholy mood, to the point of despair, I should only feel that that is a necessary mood for a poet or musician who must give so much of his inner feeling and understanding—and that it is not darkness but just another mode of expression, another view of life. . . . [3]

When I had first come aboard ship, I had looked closer at my shipmates than at our ship. I wanted to feel that some of them shared my hopes for the future. I held on to the idea of friendship and believed it was the answer to many of the ills of our world. But I had been disappointed. Weeks had passed, and my mental life was as arid as my physical one. Life had gone on, through heartaches, illness, loneliness, until the very morning of the day that was coming to a close.

The Christmas morning began auspiciously. The sea was calm, and, as the morning advanced, it took on the color of a field of lupins moving in a slight wind. I felt free of my body. The ship approached a group of islands and anchored within a few miles of one of the most beautiful of them. Scattered on the sea were other ships, a large force as we were soon to attack an island occupied by the Japanese.

My contemplation was interrupted by footsteps. I turned and saw a shipmate, unknown to me, standing near. He, too, seemed to be memorizing the scene. I spoke, and he answered with a hesitant formality which may have come from a Scandinavian inheritance. Rapport was quickly established, and our conversation ranged over a number of topics, including books and music. He left for duties and suggested that we meet again in the evening. We did. He became my best friend on the ship, and I learned eventually that he was gay, with a lover in Seattle. A sort of calm settled over me.

At twenty-nine, Rudy was closer to my age than most of the other sailors. He was getting very gray, and he had a strange mixture of tastes: Don Blanding and Willa Cather, Richard Wagner and Jeannette MacDonald. Every now and then I would read him something from Edwin's letters. He got a kick out of them and read me all of his letters, some of which were very amusing coming as they did from France and many other faraway places. Rudy and I kept up with each other through the years. Thirty-two years later, we met in London, where Edwin and I acted as tour guides for him. Later we saw him and his friend in Seattle.

There were a few others whom I enjoyed talking to, although none were as close to me as Rudy with his easygoing and good-natured manner. One of the kids was Cozy, a young nonconformer with some college education and a good vocabulary, occasionally used inaccurately. He had met some interesting people around Los Angeles, his home, and his father worked in the studios for twenty-four years. Cozy had some tales to tell and did it well. I was really surprised when he mentioned a novelist he had met, Henry Miller, that former expatriate writer of very frank novels, which were unprintable in this country at the time. Cozy was ecstatic over Duke Ellington and the not-so-well-known black singers and bands. But he was at the age where the word "bourgeoisie" crept into the conversation every so often, always disparagingly. He recalled some of my own youthful didoes.

Another shipmate with whom I spent time was Carlos, the Pharmacy Mate, who lived on a ranch near the Mexico–Texas border. He was proud and shy. Like me, Carlos was unhappy on board. His intelligence was refreshing after so much stupidity. Although we didn't see each other often, we would have long chats about books and music. He had excellent taste, and I was delighted when he mentioned as one of his favorite American writers Ellen Glasgow. I had been re-reading *A Certain Measure* so I lent it to him, and later he borrowed one of my Forster books.

One day we got to talking about books and authors. He suggested that we collaborate on a sexy novel—the *Forever Amber* sort of thing that sold so well.[4] At the time, I thought it might be fun and possibly mean a little money. We discussed plot and so forth. I began writing the opening chapter, which was pure tripe. It was hard work. It was also rather silly. "Shelly Martin" was our lady's name. Her husband dies in the war, as the story opens, and she becomes a war widow with one affair after the other. Carlos suggested a chapter in New Mexico. We had it opening in San Francisco and thence to San Antonio. But it got tiresome trying to describe a woman's breasts, and the project was eventually abandoned.

At about this time, I had an experience in which I felt that sex was in the air. I had to take a message to a handsome young officer from New Orleans with whom I had had a casual, pleasant relationship. I knocked on his living quarters, was told to come in, and delivered the message. He was lying on his bed with his jacket off. As I turned to go, he said, "Zeigler you don't have to go." I hesitated, wondering what he was suggesting but sure that I should leave quickly, which I did. Often since then I have wondered if life on the *Dickens* would have been different if I had stayed. Years later, when Edwin and I were in New Orleans, I looked him up in the telephone book—I didn't find his name.

Shortly after Christmas, we hoisted anchor and set off for Eniwetok, in the Marshall Islands. It was like a necklace of pale green stone with the stones spaced rather unevenly. The sea had gradually worn away a volcanic mountain that had once stood there. It is said to be the only perfect atoll in the world, but we didn't set foot on it.

In my spare time, I would sometimes read, although it was difficult to really enjoy anything. Edward Newbury had sent me *The History of*

Rome Hanks, which had been banned in Boston. I didn't like it very much as I have never liked to read about the Civil War. There were certain chapters that seemed awfully good, such as those dealing with a couple of rich, whorish plantation sisters. Music, too, did not bring its usual pleasures. The records were played in a noisy part of the ship, noisy because of the ventilator system, which it was so necessary to keep on. However, I did begin listening to different music such as a very good Fats Waller album, but no boogie-woogie.

Next we went to Saipan, which we had recently taken from the Japanese. We had a ringside seat to a battle, an indication of what was to come for us. One morning, the harbor was shaken with explosions as a Marine garrison on the island had cornered about 200 Japanese and was pouring mortar fire on them. Across from Saipan is Tinian. The famous 20th Air Force Super-Forts operated from these two islands. Sometimes they would take off for Japan, and we would await their return anxiously.

After taking on about 1,000 Marines along the way, we headed for the target for which we had been preparing for months, Iwo Jima. By four in the morning on Monday, February 19, we could see shells from our battleships and cruisers racing through the air before hearing their explosions. As the sun came up, Iwo Jima seemed to be just a long rock with Mount Suribachi stuck on one end. How little we knew then how much that barren waste was to cost in human life. The flag that was eventually raised was a battle flag from the *Dickens*. We had given it to the Marines of the 5th Division before they left.

The attacking planes never bothered us. Before and during the fighting, everyone aboard was very calm, and a fatalistic attitude prevailed. For a couple of days I worked about twenty hours a day but was never happier to do what little I could. I kept a sort of communication center, receiving all of the messages that came in about the various phases of the fighting and routing them to the various people who had to see them. During the day, we kept three or four messengers running about. I only had time once to watch the fighting through field glasses, and it was like seeing some grim silent movie except for the distant sounds of warfare.

I wanted to let Edwin know where I had been so I wrote in a letter, "I owe Jim a dollar. Please see that he gets it." Edwin got it. A few weeks later, I was able to give him a fuller description of the battle:

> The members of our own beach and boat party had a hell of a time on one of the two most bitterly contested beaches. . . . Our beach party went in on the sixth wave, at which time the shore is hoped to be secure enough for them to set up communications and direct the landing of supplies, etc. They were on the beach at the foot of Mt. Suribachi and were faced with intense mortar, machine gun, etc. fire. The Marines had a terrible time on that beach and our own

beach party suffered deaths and wounds. One of the radiomen died after being brought back to the ship. . . . On the fourth (I think it was) day when we heard that our flag had been raised on Suribachi we were very happy. I think Time says that the Marines wept when they raised the flag; I know I almost did when I heard that they had. . . . The beach party couldn't be relieved for a couple of days because of intense fire. If you could have seen them when they returned you would have felt like weeping. You felt that some of them would never get over what they had seen. However, time seems to heal most wounds and they are mostly back in the groove.[5]

On March 8, we crossed the Equator, and I changed from the rank of Pollywog to that of a Shellback. We had been warned some days in advance that many unpleasant things would happen to us. On the day before, Davy Jones and the various members of King Neptune's Court prepared the scene. For several days, the most open part of the deck had been prepared with a pool, a stock, and thrones for the King and his queen, princess, and baby. On the eve of the initiation, officers were made to don female garments or various combinations of clothing or lack of it. Some enlisted men did this, too. Some heads began to be shaved.

Early on that morning, we assembled on our mustering stations and bowed down to the visitors from the deep. Paddles were used on the usual places during the procedure. We were able to watch the initiation of the officers (naturally very gratifying) and then began to line up for our turns at being paddled, followed by having the Devil chase us with a small-voltage stick. Obeisance was made to the King and Queen, the Princess presented her knee to be kissed, followed by the kissing of the baby's belly. The royal baby was our butcher.

The butcher was a very fat man, the hairiest individual to be found this side of a tree in the jungle. He had rubbed on his person a paste of red pepper and vinegar. He then rubbed our faces in the mess, after which we were paddled some more as we climbed a slippery board to the pool. We had our hair cut in clumps and swatches (in my case there was so little to work on that you couldn't tell much difference when they finished), after which raw eggs were broken over our heads. Then the royal doctor shoved a thermometer dipped in some unpleasant mixture into each of our mouths and pushed us backward into the pool. We crawled out, received some more paddling and were ready to go to the head and try to clean up. I succeeded very well. It was a lot of fun, and no one was killed or missing. I had a sore spot on my ass for a few days afterward, but it was worth it.

This ritual and other smaller diversions were no doubt designed to relieve the tedium and fatigue of being at sea. Only a couple of weeks before, I had written Edwin in one of my lowest states of mind I had at sea:

> Anger seethes and then it settles down and the refuse floats away. But it comes like those geysers in our western parks that spurt so often that you never know when to expect them to flare up. I can put up with many things, but I cannot bear a certain attitude of mind, an arrogance born of ignorance, a patronage born of position. I have been made almost blindly angry today, as you have guessed. I see others about me, perhaps as angry, and I try to soothe them. But who is to soothe me?[6]

In that same letter, though, I relayed to Edwin an amusing anecdote that I hoped lightened it a bit:

> Someone stole a large cake made for the Captain the other day. The radiomen got the blame but I finally convinced the persons making the accusation that we hadn't even had a piece of the damn cake. I listened to a lecture on stealing (not directed at me) and several threats and ended convinced that if I ever saw such a cake I would most certainly steal it.[7]

On April 1 we took part in our second big adventure of the war, an attack on Okinawa. The radio officer had decided that radiomen would be the saviors of the ship if all other ratings were killed. We, therefore, had to perform other duties from time to time. My turn to steer the ship came on the midnight we were steaming toward Okinawa in a large convoy of ships, all in total darkness. I had been given no instructions and had never paid any attention to the wheel. I didn't even know how to drive a car! As soon as I took over the wheel and began turning it in the wrong direction the Captain yelled, "Who the hell is on the wheel, get him off!" Radiomen performed only their own skills from then on.

It was Easter Sunday. About 500 men gathered on the deck for the Chaplain's message bringing the beauty of Easter to the sincere, worshipping men to whom death was an imminent possibility. The Chaplain told us later that he wouldn't have traded his place that morning for the greatest pulpit on Earth. Though casualties were high with the American forces, the fighting was less severe than at Iwo Jima. Wanting to let Edwin know where I had been, I made a foolish statement in a letter and said, "But, it's okay in a way." He got it.

Between such engagements, we had a rather settled routine. There always was work on the *Dickens*: painting the ship, scraping, loading, unloading. There was never any let-up, except sometimes on Sunday at sea, where a holiday routine prevailed. Of course, radiomen stood watches the same all of the time. We were even busier in port, for then we had mail coming in. One of my letters to Edwin captured some of the experiences:

> This is one of those days when the whole vast Pacific seems to crowd in on me and add its weight to the sun's heat. A mad watch in the morning, then an afternoon moving from one uncomfortable position to another, trying to escape the sun, the noise of paint being chipped, of pneumatic drills, of commands, of people talking to me. After chow I helped in the shack a while, typing the news and routing some messages. . . . The moon has risen quite a bit already. It is between two little spots of land with a long bank of clouds underneath. Last night was beautiful. . . . This is the first time I've tried writing a letter by moonlight. It is terribly hot below and I've got to try to get some sleep soon for I go on watch at 1:30 A.M. and know I won't sleep again until 2 the following morning. I cannot sleep during the day in the insufferable heat.[8]

There were breaks from this routine and the heat. Once we anchored near some beautiful islands and were allowed to go ashore for swimming, even though it was raining. The branches of the trees extended over the water, in which we felt exhilaratingly alive, cavorting like children. A few natives appeared from time to time, no doubt thinking us mad. Years later, Edwin and I were having dinner with a young couple who had been bookstore customers before they became friends. During an evening of conversation, I learned that the young officer in charge of that beach party was the very man now sitting across from us with his lovely wife.

Toward the end of April, I awoke from a bit of sleep after a midnight-to-six duty with an excruciating pain. I didn't want to die on my top bunk, so I found my way to the dispensary in my underwear and fainted as I entered the door. For a week I stayed there, kidney stones refusing to leave their comfortable berth. On May 5th, I was transferred to the base hospital on Guam, one of many such facilities scattered around the Pacific.

I had freedom of movement and enjoyed the leisure while waiting for a stone or stones to pass. I filtered my urine through a piece of gauze, hoping to catch the elusive devils. Often I walked in the neighborhood, admiring the golden-brown Chamorros who tended their small garden or watered their stock knowing that they were now safe. The light was clear and pale in the morning, and I remember the flame trees that seemed to burn.

At the hospital, with the radio kept low most of the time, and reasonably good food, I was feeling better, despite the dilemma that brought me here. I could think more clearly about the future. I wrote Edwin about the possibility of opening a bookstore in the basement of my family home, 9 College Street.

> I have been laying here today thinking or wondering if you would care to have a book and record shop in the old kitchen and stable

under the low part of the house. We could do whatever we liked with the place, have living quarters there, and do something with the yard. The complications of family could be kept to a minimum I believe. . . . If we had the bookshop, could we not build a place on an acreage somewhere near the city in our spare time?[9]

The advantages, I explained, would be many as it was across the street from the College of Charleston, and my aunts would be very receptive.

On May 19, the stones gave up their haven, and, next day, I was pronounced fit to travel, though this base did not know where my ship was. I was sent to the makeshift base in Saipan, recently secured, and lingered there for a few days as the officers there didn't know where the *Dickens* was either. Perhaps it was in Manila. I persuaded a seaplane pilot to take me with his crew there.

Manila's harbor was a tangle of sunken ships, the city under occasional pockets of resistance. As we came close to the city, we could see the destruction increasing as we went up the Pasig River, which was like a canal cutting through the ruins. As soon as we docked, we were set upon by Filipinos who wanted to buy or sell. The streets were littered with debris among which drifted Japanese money. Hurrying Filipinos were everywhere, gathering wood or tin or pasteboard and carrying incredible bundles on their heads or backs. I saw shops without roofs, stumps of trees, churches without steeples or domes. Occasionally, a shot would ring out in the distance. The scene filled me with awe. Even though most of what we saw was in ruins, there was an air of grandeur.

At the receiving station, I was told that they had no idea where the *Dickens* might be. I could try Subic Bay, which we were just beginning to develop. That night, I got on a riverboat, pulled a blanket out of my sea bag, and lay on the deck hoping for sleep that never came. As dawn approached, I gazed out at the huts on stilts in the water, some residents already up and attending to fishing boats. The trip was hot and uncomfortable in the crowded little boat that followed the mountainous coastline before entering a small river. Naked children played in the mud.

Conditions were primitive at the Subic Bay station, the most recently captured place in which I had been. There was a stench in the mud that was everywhere. I went immediately to headquarters. They didn't know where the ship was either. I was assigned to a tent where I was pleased to find a black sailor from Charleston with whom I could talk about our Lowcountry.

I was to report to a group that was making gardens around the officers' quarters since I had a "light duty" slip. That didn't appeal to me, so I goofed off as much as possible. After a couple of weeks, I saw three men from the *Dickens* come ashore. I ran to them and learned that the ship had been in harbor for two weeks. I gathered my gear, jumped in the boat with them, and returned to the *Dickens*. If I had been more adventurous I might still be roaming around somewhere in the Pacific.

I was not to remain long on the ship, but it was good to see old friends such as Rudy and Carlos as well as to go through the stack of mail that had been waiting for me. In one letter, George informed me about a disturbing event that happened to two civil-service employees who were "roommates," one of whom, Stuart, was a clerk in George's office. "His roommate has been discharged from the government service and Stuart feels that he will be next, so he is resigning. . . . I am very unhappy about it and regret the unhealthy Victorian standards."[10] Although this pattern would become prevalent after the war, neither I nor friends such as Rudy or Carlos faced any problems while in service.

Kidney stones appeared again, and it was decided that I should be sent to the hospital on Manus, in the Admiralty Islands off the coast of New Guinea. All that I knew of that island was that Margaret Mead had done anthropological work there. She didn't like Manus society, which she found materialistic, puritanical, and with sexual double standards —the latter a particular bête noir to that brilliant and sexually free woman.

As it turned out, in the month that I was there in the hospital, up and about every day, waiting, I was only able to observe one native closely. He was a very dark man, not quite five feet tall. He was in the bed next to mine. We couldn't communicate except through smiles and gestures. He had chosen to be a runner for us in the deep wood among the corded vines. When shrapnel tore his legs, he crawled back to this place, coral-torn from feet to face. He seemed very happy to be sharing white sheets and ice cream every day.

As time passed, I hadn't heard from Edwin about the plans for the bookstore since his letters hadn't arrived. I was exchanging letters with George, and, in mid-July, I wrote him:

> I know we are both anxious to be independent. . . . I think the work would be agreeable to both of us. I could write in the mornings and take over in the afternoon, when Edwin could garden. . . . By having a basement apartment we would be independent of the family, you can understand that it would be best to have a separate establishment. . . . I want to know his honest reaction. If I could just get some back mail![11]

On the other side of the world, George was writing me, as he sometimes did, about his gay friends or experiences in Washington. One of his young friends, Frank, had recently been released from a prisoner-of-war camp in Germany. George had been worried about him for months. When he returned to the States, the two picked up correspondence and then planned to meet at summer's end. However, George also received a phone call from a former office boy, now a corporal stationed in Virginia, as a chaplain's assistant, "and was almost in tears because he hadn't heard from Frank, whom he adores over-much. So I am between two fires for possibly Frank is trying to withdraw from an embarrassing situation."[12] In that same letter, George also described his "babe in the woods" outlook after learning that

> right over the restaurant where I have been lunching all this time was a "twenty-dollar minimum" establishment for "physiotherapy" and so forth. The raid took place last Friday and not since reaching the last book of Marcel Proust have I read of this particular brand of establishment. It was one devoted to the enjoyments peculiar to the Marquis de Sade, and leather belts, ropes, and long bamboo rods were much in evidence (as were two "high officials" in the government). . . .

Meanwhile, sailors came and went from the Manus hospital. I didn't make any real friends. At night, I would often hear a truck drive up to the hut beyond my window to deliver the dead. More pleasant sounds were the jungle noises that began as darkness came on. These were sounds that a modern composer might use. The days seemed endless during that month until one day when a doctor said that I should have a kidney operation. "What will happen after the operation?" I asked. "Oh, I'm afraid you would have to get out of the service." With joy, I said "Operate tomorrow."

After a week recovering, I was put on a hospital ship bound for San Francisco. The return trip across the Pacific was different. The sea was calm. I lay on the deck sunbathing. I ate well, and there were attentive corpsmen. The Japanese surrender occurred while we were en route, traveling unescorted the 5,750 miles. After almost a month, I arrived in San Francisco with a three-day liberty before heading for the East Coast and freedom.

On August 21, we arrived about 6 P.M. at the U.S. Navy Receiving Hospital. I was able to make long-distance phone calls to my family and to George. The connection to George was clearer, and it only took forty-five minutes to get my call to him. At 11:45 in the evening, George's phone rang. He was ecstatic!

I spent some time trying to call Mrs. Schwab, but there was no phone in her name, so I sent her a telegram, but with no response. We didn't get liberty until the next day when, following our plan, I went to her apartment house and asked if there was any news of Edwin or a message for me. She had given Edwin a little apartment in the basement. He was out buying groceries but soon returned. We forgot all about food. He was the same dear Edwin except for the hearing aid, which he wore as though it were a natural part of his body and not a burden.

Mrs. Schwab was nice to us. She gave Edwin sheets, though he was supposed to furnish them, and brought us peaches. Edwin gave up his job the day before he heard from me as it entailed climbing telephone poles and cutting down tree limbs. He would get another job when I left.

During the seventy-two hours that we had together, our first outdoor activity was going to the splendid market nearby and stocking up on fruits and vegetables (Edwin made me drink quantities of milk and eat fruit between meals) that I hadn't had in some time. Except for one meal of Mrs. Helvig's chicken pie, we cooked in, and I felt that I was beginning to gain back pounds lost at sea. When Edwin and I said goodbye at the railroad station, we embraced and parted without the pain of former leavings. We knew we would be together again soon.

I went to Fort Eustis, Virginia for the last formalities of my service before going to the navy base at Charleston for a health evaluation and termination on November 2, 1945. The last letter I wrote while in the service was that of October 24, from the Receiving Station at Norfolk, telling George, "I am leaving at five tomorrow for Charleston and the open road to freedom and I'm light headed at the thoughts that flit through my addled pate. It shouldn't take but a few days to be separated at the Charleston Receiving Station. Hurrah!"[13]

That fall, George visited 9 College Street in Charleston. He helped me organize my best poems for a possible book, had quiet conversations with me (sharing with me his desire to retire soon and live near Edwin and me), and enjoyed touring the city and the nearby countryside. Near the end of his stay, he wrote Edwin: "The success of your bookshop will influence many lives. I hope it will make you and John happy." Commenting on the "strangely provincial aspects of the place," George noted

> a lack of things here. Bookstores, for instance. The two now functioning are pretty bad. . . . Even decent eating places. Would the supply of these things be appreciated and supported? Or are the reflections on the utter all-rightness of one's ancestors sufficient to entertain, instruct, and provide growth to one's soul? Do come back and make the effort to provide a meeting place for the young would-be seekers after food for the mind and the spirit and the soul. . . . [14]

George also penned me a letter, with a warning that "Now that I've seen 9 College Street . . . the house is stronger than any of its occupants. Will it be possible for you actually to slip away from the quarters for your writing?"[15]

Edwin departed San Francisco and his job in the Oreo factory around the end of November. As my status was uncertain, we had decided that he might as well remain there to work and to haunt the bookshops, since we had decided that our bookstore would have a combination of new and used books. He arrived by bus in Charleston on December 5, stopping in

Pasadena and Tulsa to see sisters and then on to Thomasville for a visit with his mother.

While waiting for his arrival, my Aunt Peggy thought I needed a special holiday, with big-city excitement. She took me to New York for theater and a Wagnerian opera—a stimulation that made me quite ready to greet Edwin and plan for what would be known as The Book Basement. Sitting near an oil heater listening to Mozart on the Victrola, I wrote to George on business stationery that was already printed, recounting: "The women had such tremendous bosoms, mostly encased in filmy black lace. About eight of them marching across the stages was a wonderful sight, comic but sort of gorgeous. A dairyman would have loved it, and put them out to pasture."[16]

Part III
Book Basement, Travels, and Beyond

13 The Book Basement Years

Edwin arrived in Charleston in early December, and we immediately started renovating the large room beyond the bookshop's single room and rectangular hall. We would have a bed-sitting room, small kitchen, and bath there. Then we began painting, Edwin repaired the floor in the bathroom, and we built bookshelves in the room where my great aunts had had a private school for over thirty years. Two of the desks used by their students would be bins for inexpensive books on the College Street sidewalk in the front of the shop. There was a very attractive, mid-nineteenth-century mantel and fireplace with two brown wicker chairs with yellow and wine cushions for browsers, a small Indian rug in front of the hearth, and my old brown imitation leather chest by one of the windows near the wine cellar. Edwin soon had the garden in good shape, and there were comfortable chairs on the patio, beneath an upstairs porch. Camellias and azaleas were planted as well as a dogwood tree, and the wisteria that climbed up to the third floor of the house was carefully manicured.

We had just over 2,000 dollars in savings with which to order stock. Edwin and I pored over catalogues, searching out basic stock items. Our own libraries would fill up many shelves and serve as the nucleus of our second-hand department. We had a desk, a typewriter, and a metal box that would be our till. No adding machine or other fancy gadgets.

Writing to George Scheirer, I told him of the excitement about the bookstore, "There are people in Charleston who long to feel a breath of fresh air and I think they consider that they are going to find a little of it here."[1] He had made arrangements for a handsome sign to be designed and made in Washington. When drying, the sign—THE BOOK BASEMENT—was sitting in the showroom of the International Galleries. George wrote us that "many people have asked where this bookshop is located. When the reply was 'Charleston, South Carolina,' one fellow said, 'It must be Zeigler.'"[2] The speaker was the artist Phillip Bell.[3]

Prentiss Taylor, a well-known lithographer, was another person who happened by the gallery when George was there. I had first met Prentiss in Washington at Perks' apartment in 1935. He was already a well-known

Figure 13.1 Edwin and John at front of The Book Basement.

figure in Washington's art circles because of his accomplished lithographs, some of which had been done after two summers in Charleston at the Pink House, which his friend Josephine Pinckney had asked friends to loan him. He was the most cosmopolitan of our group, with friends such as Carl Van Vechten, Aaron Copland, Rachel Field, and Langston Hughes.[4] In the diaries that Prentiss kept while working as an art therapist at St. Elizabeth's Hospital, he details many sessions with Ezra Pound and social meetings with his wife and son. Pound was surprised to find in him an intellectual with whom he could talk of literature and art. Prentiss visited Charleston in the middle of March and made a beautiful drawing of the front of the shop, which we used as a postcard for twenty-five years.

When shipping the sign to us, George asked us to accept it with the hope that it "may always be near your doorway and bring you luck and happiness." Alas, my aunt found it too large for the house, and we only used it at book fairs.

We opened The Book Basement on Carson McCullers' birthday—February 19, 1946. In early March, she wrote Edwin, whom she always addressed in letters as "Precious," that she was "greatly touched when you wrote that it was not altogether an accident that the first day of the shop was my birthday." So, on that day, "We had a toast to the bookshop. We imagined how the place looked and what the opening was like." She told us of her hopes to visit soon, perhaps by boat from Boston, along with news that publication of *The Member of the Wedding*, which was "so damned difficult to write," would be delayed until March 19. That visit never materialized, but she and Reeves would spend time with us and enjoy the bookshop two years later. However, we placed four copies of Carson's book in our display window along with her picture, although, as I confided in George at the time, I didn't expect her third novel to be very popular there.[5]

The local newspaper had a pleasant article about us and the opening of the shop, and relatives and friends were on hand to bid us success. I can still visualize our first customers the next day. A College of Charleston professor, his wife, and little daughter each bought a book; a nurse bought something; and a man who continued as a customer until we sold the shop bought used books. Laura Bragg, whom I had first met when I was a student at The Citadel, inviting me into her literary world, also sent people our way.

We didn't know it at the time, but the visit to the shop one day of two Belgians from a freighter in harbor would add greatly to the friendships we would make in Antwerp. These young men asked if there was anywhere in Charleston where they could hear music. There wasn't, so we asked them to come by that evening to listen to records. They not only came that night but several following until their ship left port. One of them would return to Charleston years later as captain of his own ship, and we would take Charles to dinner and have champagne on the ship at midnight, just before departure. Meanwhile, we exchanged Christmas greetings and, a few years later, visited Antwerp, where we were made welcome by all of the extended family of Charles, who was at sea. For two days, we were wined and dined, driven to other cities, by a younger brother and his fiancée, who, through the years, would exchange visits with us, becoming our closest European friends. As we entered a cellar bar one night, the orchestra began playing "Carolina Moon." We were assured that this was a coincidence and not arranged previously.

Another interesting sailor also became a good friend. As we were leaving a movie theater one night in winter, a young man also came out and began talking with us about the movie. Al was a sailor in civilian clothes. He walked along with us as far as the bookstore, as he wanted to know where it was. Al soon began to be a regular in the shop, and we were charmed by his intelligence and enthusiasm.

When George visited in the spring, the four of us spent a weekend at Sullivan's Island, and George fell under the spell of Al, too. I think he regarded us as two nice old uncles who made him feel at home. The thought of sex never entered into our heads. On a weekend visit to Charlotte to see Bob and Ed, he came into my single bed to evade the advances of Bob, and we slept quietly side by side.

By the next fall, he was assigned to another post, and we didn't see him again until about thirty-five years later when he knocked on our door, in his fifties, a college history professor. He had matured, but he was still lovable, and we had a lovely afternoon and evening together.

Customers seemed to value Edwin's humor as well as the opportunity to leisurely browse the shelves. One day, a woman from out of town asked Edwin, "Do you know Mrs. Verner's *Mellowed by Time*?" He replied, "She is?" Another woman whom we had never seen came in and immediately asked Edwin if he had been born again. "No, Madame," he replied, "Once was enough."

Before long, the college librarian began buying books from us. This was followed over the next few years by librarians from across the state coming to us for Caroliniana, as we eventually kept about 600 titles in stock. Our lending library was also widely used. Within the first week, we had twenty-three books in circulation and, as time went on, found these brought people in fairly often.

Soon after our opening we joined the N.A.A.C.P. On the U.S.S. *Dickens* I had often gone up on the Captain's deck. Outside of his quarters, I would talk with his black steward, who would sometimes bring me a leftover pork chop or piece of cake from the Captain's table. The rating of steward, or servant, was the only one available to a black sailor. Because of our growing friendship, I was sometimes called a "Nigger lover." It was probably because of this that we joined the organization.

We also became members of an interracial group, where we met our first liberal Charlestonians, who would become good friends and customers.[6] Our aim was to get black policemen on the force. We finally succeeded in getting two added to what was an all-white force. Decades later, we had a black police chief who was sought after by many large cities.

We had warm relationships with black librarians and principals who worked in the area's segregated school systems. Often we had book fairs in their schools where parents would buy books for the libraries, and the library also would receive some of the proceeds of the sales. Years earlier, Laura Bragg, who was in charge of the Charleston Museum, had arranged for traveling exhibits to these all-black schools as well as opening up the museum to black patrons and helping to establish the city's first free library.[7]

Soon, too, Edwin and I began to meet other gay men who formed a small and invisible community. Our closest gay friends were Kip and Jerry.[8] We met them at a pub-restaurant where they were seated with an older gay friend of ours. He came over to greet us and then introduced us to the couple who were about ten years younger than us. We were asked if we played bridge, and, within a week, we were visiting back and forth for games. When they discovered a small house with ten acres for sale across the river in what was then the isolated town of Mount Pleasant, we joined them on a Sunday and helped paint one side of the house, pictures of which were shown to enable them to get an F.H.A. loan. Later we helped plant 1,000 pine trees in the mostly barren acreage. When they moved to New York City for business reasons and rented their place, we kept up with each other by visits. When they moved back in the 1970s, parties were quieter, and Jerry became well known as a rose and camellia expert.

My friends Nell and Perks came for visits, sometimes together. They became great favorites of the family. Carter never visited, and the last time I saw him was in London when we dined together and went to a play. He was in his sixties, and our relationship was such as it had always been. My last evening with Perks was at a dinner party in Washington whose host we had never met. It was a happy evening with several old friends from my Washington days. Sadly, neither Perks nor Carter were letter-writers.

Although there were a few "mixed bars" in Charleston, such as Club 49, the Cove, and the Elbow Cocktail Lounge, we preferred to spend our time at people's homes. We would play bridge and attend parties. At some of those parties in the country was an air-force lieutenant. Someone in our group had given the names of all of us who had attended parties, and, one day, a couple of air-force investigators came into the shop to talk with me. They assured me that I was not under investigation but that they wanted to find out more about this young officer. They asked how I met him. I said that my aunt and I had gone to the First Baptist Church and heard him in *The Messiah* and that we talked with him afterward. "Did you ever entertain him," asked one of the stern-looking investigators. "Yes," I replied. "My aunt and uncle invited him to Sullivan's Island where we were staying." While I kept trying to place him in respectable and innocuous situations, the investigators persisted with their line of questions. "Did you ever see him in drag?" I responded curtly, "Never." They left without thanking me.

Although the young lieutenant was eventually charged by the Air Force with homosexual activity, they were never able to prove any of the allegations against him. But, for the rest of his term in the service, he was not assigned duties. However, he was able to get two further degrees on the G.I. Bill and would become head of the history department in a fine college following his discharge.

Of course, many gay men who had served honorably during the war did not fare as well. But the presence of so many service men in Charleston's naval and air-force bases made connections with some of them inevitable. Since I was self-employed, it never bothered me that investigators came once to visit, but with others, like Jerry, who was a retired officer, it created more concerns. Of course, there were other naval and air men who identified as straight but did engage in homosexual activity. This, too, sometimes created problems, the most infamous being the so-called Candle Stick Murder Case. This involved an eighteen-year-old air-force man who bludgeoned a gay man, Jack Dobbins, with an antique brass candlestick from the thirty-year-old's Queen Street bedroom fireplace mantel. We didn't know the young man but were incensed at the negative publicity he received. A Citadel professor, whose name was found in the victim's notebook, was questioned and allowed to resign without dishonor.[9]

These incidents, though, occurred in the 1950s at a time when McCarthyism and the Cold War had created a climate of intolerance toward minorities of any type. However, immediately after the war, a more liberal attitude seemed to prevail, at least nationally. Books by homosexual writers Tennessee Williams and Gore Vidal were reviewed favorably in *Life* and *Newsweek*. Naturally, we stocked such books as *Other Voices, Other Rooms* and *City and the Pillar*, but there never was much interest in them. We had more business selling bestsellers, children's books, Caroliniana, and out-of-print books.

In 1947, the College asked us if we would sell their textbooks, which they would order and buy, as they had no facility at the time. We agreed. Not only would we get a percentage of the sales but it would also mean that every student would become familiar with our shop. To make room for the textbooks, we built shelves in the rectangular hall.

Although much of our time during that first year or two was devoted to renovations and business, Edwin and I each had time for our individual pursuits—something which we both recognized was important for our relationship. Some of my poetry, written earlier, found publishers. George continued to send manuscripts of *The Two Cubs*, but rejections always followed, sometimes with words like "pleasant," or "well-written."

When George showed the story to Munro Leaf, author of *The Story of Ferdinand*, he predicted that *The Two Cubs* would be the next Ferdinand.[10] Leaf told the editor of the *Charleston News and Courier* that he had read a children's story by a South Carolinian that could become a bestseller. That editor was telling my father this one day when my father responded, "That's my son!" During these years, I rarely wrote, being busy, happy, and without the need to express myself except to Edwin and the bookstore.

Edwin's hobby at this time was gardening, but his passion was classical music. Our living quarters were usually flooded with beautiful sounds, and, on Saturdays, when the Metropolitan Opera was broadcasting, the shop was alive with its sounds. We went to every classical music concert, but the city offered few in those years. In the shop, we tended to take on duties for which we were best suited. Edwin paid more attention to the Carolinian department, going each year to the annual library meetings, where he would display books and hand out mimeographed sheets of our holdings. I would usually wait on customers because of my better hearing, and I did the accounting and ordering. We never had any disputes about the shop or about anything else in our lives, both of us growing into our life together naturally.

Figure 13.2 Edwin shelving at The Book Basement.

Both Edwin and I had grown up in loving families, and neither of us had ever been jealous or had ugly moments with our sisters and brother. We had grown up in harmony with our loved ones, and that harmony was maintained in our relationship. He would go to visit his mother in Thomasville from time to time, and sometimes I would be able to go with him. I was accepted as one of the family, as he was accepted and loved by all of my relatives. On many Sundays we would go to visit my parents, who lived about thirty miles away. Summers were spent at the beach with my aunt and her husband, and we always had dinner together during the week in the dining room of 9 College Street. My nieces and nephews and their children were often with us.

Within a year, our business had grown to the point that we moved our living quarters upstairs so that we could build shelves and turn the back-room, which had a graceful mantel and fireplace, into a lending library and children's book room. With a kitchen nearby, we could offer favored customers tea. When a mother would come in with a little girl, I would call the child "Hepsibah," and she would predictably say that wasn't her name. On cue, I would respond, telling her that when she was in the shop that would be her name. Having eleven nieces and nephews, I was used to talking with children, and I had learned that they liked the unexpected. Thirty years later, a young woman, serving punch at a library function, said to me, "Mr. Zeigler, I'm Hepsibah."

Books for children were quite popular as were out-of-print books. When I was about eighty-five, I read an article by an antiquarian dealer in Denver who said that when he was ten years old he requested two kindly old gentlemen at The Book Basement to find him a certain book, which they did, charging him one dollar. He said that it was because of his early experiences in the shop that he eventually opened his own place. I smiled, remembering him as a boy and us being only in our early forties.

Early in the 1950s, we were able, at last, to make an extended holiday. We went to Mexico in the old Ford, which had been over 150,000 miles, and spent an exciting month exploring that interesting country, buying cheap pottery and glass for the beach house. In Mexico City, at the end of our explorations, we were looking at ceramics in a window when history repeated itself. A handsome young Mexican, about thirty, began talking to us in good English. He was a history high-school teacher. After preliminaries, he asked if he could go back to our hotel with us. Edwin and I looked at each other, smiled, and said yes. I think that we both thought that the experience would be a proper ending to our visit in this fascinating country. And it was! He was our guide to the city for the next two days, and, for years, we exchanged Christmas greetings.

We often took a brief holiday between Christmas and New Year's, when business was slow, leaving our college student help in charge of the shop. We went several times to pre-Castro Cuba, where we stayed in Havana at the hotel where Hemingway had written one of his novels. We would spend the days on the beach and the evenings having Cuba Libras for twenty-five cents at Hemingway's favorite bar. On a couple of occasions, we stayed at a beach resort out of Havana in a guest house run by a couple of middle-aged gay Cubans. Havana seemed a city open to anything one might desire, with an intangible air of corruption.[11]

Eventually we had money enough for trips to Europe, and London became a base from which we would go to other countries. Bookstore friends in London often lent us an extra flat they owned. It was next to the flat where Radclyffe Hall and Una Troubridge had lived.[12] It was only later that we developed gay friendships in London and on the Continent. On some European trips, we took my Aunt Peggy and Edwin's sister Marjorie, or my sister Virginia. There were the usual sightseeing holidays in England, Scotland, Ireland, France, and Denmark.

During the nearly twenty-five years we operated The Book Basement we had many interesting customers and met other bookstore proprietors. Once two small girls cried as they left the shop telling their mother that those men didn't have a bed to sleep on! In the early spring of 1954, the wonderful children's author, Maurice Sendak, became a customer while staying with a friend at DuBose Heyward's old home on Folly Beach. He asked us to try to find old children's books which he wanted for their illustrations, which we did. Later, upon his return to New York, he wrote: "It's fun making new friends quickly without the usual fuss and feathers. . . . Harper's is snapping the whip over my back to get the book done."[13]

Perhaps our strangest customer was a former history professor at the College who had been dismissed after one year. He told his students one day that the Chinese were going to take over the United States by dropping 100,000 pregnant women over the country. Their children would be the "fifth column" to take over America. On this visit, he had with him his wife, bedraggled and in bedroom slippers, who claimed to be Anastasia, daughter of the murdered czar. Her claim was eventually disproved by DNA testing. She looked like something out of *Tobacco Road*.

We also became good friends with other booksellers, as we all subscribed to *Antiquarian Bookman*, where we advertised for out-of-print books. We met our first London bookseller when a Charleston serviceman gave our name to a bookstore proprietor who began ordering U.S. publications. We, in turn, ordered English books from him and, when we next visited London, became acquainted with the young woman with a library-science degree who was the shop's mainstay. She and her future husband became our closest friends in London and often visited us in Charleston in the 1970s.

Besides the warm friendships that sprang up with customers, especially those from the area who found the shop a quiet, literary haven, we also always had a good college student to help us out, particularly when we took a holiday, as we often did between Christmas and New Year when business was slow. One of those young men, David Heisser, would later be a librarian at The Citadel. He entered the College of Charleston in 1960 and often found himself visiting our shop, "perhaps more like haunting it, perusing the books," he later wrote to us. Eventually, he worked part-time as a clerk, often alongside Laura Bragg, with whom he enjoyed a morning ritual of coffee followed by discussing a book one or the other was reading. "Everybody in Charleston who had a brain turned up in the shop and most of them were happy to chat. Boredom was impossible." He relayed one anecdote to us when he clerked as we were taking a holiday:

> A minister of some congregation from one of the remoter parts of the islands—Wadmalaw I think—arrived in a long black car, dressed head-to-toe in black. He was there to pick up a book he'd had specially ordered. It was a tome from some obscure press giving precise instructions for conjuring Satan. The minister paid in cash and departed without a word. . . . [14]

Our shop at 9 College Street also hosted many autographing parties for local authors. The first one was held in August 1946. John Bennett signed copies of his latest book, *Doctor to the Dead: Grotesque Legends and Folk Tales of Old Charleston*, as did Frances Mazo Butwin, whose translations of the short stories of Sholem Aleichem had just been published as *The Old Country*. Bennett, whom I met when I was first introduced to the Poetry Society of South Carolina, was now eighty years old. I also had known Frances Mazo Butwin for many years as she had been editor of the College of Charleston's magazine when I was editor of The Citadel's *Shako*. Autograph parties were held subsequently for Josephine Pinckney, Drayton Mayrant, Mrs. Mark Clark, and others.

We never had such a party for Carson McCullers. She and Reeves first visited our family home in May 1948 and went on to stay for a time at a rented beach house on Sullivan's Island. Reeves took care of Carson's personal needs while they enjoyed various members of my family, the ones living in the house and those popping in from other places. Sullivan's Island was quieter, and we were visited there by Bob and Edward, whom Carson had not seen since Bob's tour of duty at Fort Benning.

Carson's weakened limbs were helped by the sun and sea, into which she immersed herself each day. Prone to illness, when she became feverish, she decided to return to Nyack, where her doctor diagnosed her as having 'flu.

It seemed to me that Carson and Reeves were still very much in love. Reeves had given up drinking and went to an AA meeting. Carson was proud of him and his exemplary military record as a Ranger in France. After Reeves' death by suicide in France, where they were living in the

Figure 13.3 (From left to right) Edward N., John, Bob, Carson, Edwin, Reeves, Charleston, 1948.

spring of 1954, Carson visited us for a month. She liked to sit in the little kitchen of the bookstore and read, sometimes sipping Scotch, sometimes talking to students.

Toward the end of her visit, she was agreeable to meeting some of our friends at a party on the patio by the garden. She had already met Laura

Bragg and Kip and Jerry. That afternoon, she met Hilda and Robert Marks, the latter a writer and former Charlestonian now living in New York. Hilda was born in Austria and had been a refugee from the Nazis. After her return to New York, they became two of her closest friends, Hilda becoming especially close. Robert would be a pallbearer for both her mother and herself. From Charleston, Carson went first to Charlotte to visit Bob and Edward.

On April 12, 1963, Carson made her last visit to Charleston with her friend Dr. Mary Mercer, a charming and beautiful woman of our age. They had to stay at a hotel because Carson could not manage stairs. This was a quiet, thoughtful visit as Dr. Mercer, a child psychiatrist, had brought peace of mind to Carson. Three and a half years later, after being comatose for forty-nine days, Carson died on September 29, 1967. Edwin took the night train to New York to attend the funeral. Her death had been expected, and Edwin's grief, as well as mine, was lessened by the knowledge that she was no longer suffering. She had always been a good and loving friend to us and had always borne her illnesses with bravery.

Before Carson's death, our greatest loss was the death of George Scheirer, who died of a sudden heart attack in 1959 in the charming house he had bought in Bethesda upon his retirement nine years earlier. Although this most compassionate and loving of human beings never came to live with us, he visited on occasion, and his correspondence after the war years was steady. We often visited him and his sister, Nellian. During retirement, George had more time to spend bookbinding and teaching about the process but had mostly enjoyed listening to Saturday-afternoon Metropolitan Opera, attending an occasional concert or theater production, playing the piano, studying foreign languages, and, of course, reading and corresponding with his friends. On his last birthday, he had written to me:

> The only excuse for growing older and older and older is, I suppose, the possibility of making some worthwhile contribution for the benefit of man or the development of friendship in all its possibilities. Since, alas, I have no contributions to make, I linger on for the sake of friendship.[15]

We drove to Washington to be with Nellian. George had left me all of his books, including those he had bound beautifully through his Rabbit Hutch Bindery, but I did not remove them from their home until she died in 1974. When we returned from the funeral, there was a letter from George in the mailbox. He had written it the night he died, before a second heart attack. He had placed it in the mail slot where it was picked up the morning after his death. It spoke of a near death experience he had just had. After his death, his name was entered in the Book of Memory in the National Cathedral, a distinguished honor for an outstanding citizen

Figure 13.4 Carson, Edwin, and John, 1954, Charleston.

of Washington. In the years that followed, several Charleston cultural institutions had exhibits of his fine bindings.

In 1970, we were informed by the College of Charleston that it had been permitted to buy up the block on which we were located. That coincided with the twenty-fifth anniversary of the opening of The Book Basement. We hosted a celebration party for our most treasured heterosexual customers on one night and for about twenty gay friends the next evening. At the second party, there was a Baptist minister and a Catholic priest. The priest, who was a teacher, brought another priest who had, for the past two years, been a female impersonator in a Miami club.

Although events such as Stonewall and gay liberation had not yet entered the consciousness of most in Charleston's gay community, it was far from being an inhospitable place for homosexuals. Often in the winter, wealthy and retired gay couples came to Charleston and were accepted into local society because of their "credentials." They were usually referred to simply as "the boys." As the years have passed, I have often thought back to social gatherings, warm friendships, and quiet acceptance from heterosexuals, wondering what all of the fuss was about.

I would like to emphasize that among about twenty-five gay couples whom Edwin and I knew intimately, almost all living in Southern cities, none had any problems with their identity as homosexuals. They were lawyers, teachers, doctors, architects, bankers, artists, and a couple of ministers. None suffered discrimination, nor did careers suffer. None actually came "out of the closet," but, because of their lifestyles, staying with the same partner for twenty-five to fifty years, their same-sex arrangements were obviously known. None of these friends ever had any problem about being accepted by relatives.

I think the myth that all of the homosexuals of my time had a hard time because of being gay should be dispelled. We all hated the word "queer," which among things means "shady," of a questionable nature. We felt that being homosexual was perfectly normal for us as human beings who were born with our natures as some were born left-handed or bow-legged.

Just before we learned of the College's intention, my aunt Peggy died, leaving me the house. Edwin and I began looking for something I could afford and eventually found a house in such bad condition that it took seven months to renovate. In early 1971, we sold The Book Basement and retired, not wanting to continue in an ordinary sort of store where the ambience would not be the same. A new life of leisure and extensive travels would begin while The Book Basement fell into oblivion as the new owners, with drugs and alcohol playing their part, built up debts that forced the store's closing a couple of years later.

Figure 13.5 The Book Basement. Etching by Prentiss Taylor.

14 Last Years

Before moving into our new home, built in 1846 but completely renovated, there was all of the furniture and "stuff" that we didn't need to be disposed of. Nieces and nephews came, and a friend arranged for a garage sale. My family had lived for ninety-six years in that very large house at 9 College Street.

My aunt had given me her beach house at Sullivan's Island a couple of years before she died, and we spent most of the late spring and summer months there. As we both had numerous younger relatives, there were island guests most summers. Our two families were like one big happy family, and, while nothing was ever talked about as to our sexuality, we were sure that the older relatives understood our relationship. We kept the beach house until 1983, when it had become a burden because of the large yard which required frequent mowing and the house that began to need painting and repairs. We sold it, without regret, always looking forward rather than backward.

In 1973, I was in London for a while without Edwin. Missing him, I decided to go to a bath just a few blocks from the apartment in which I was staying. It was a decorous place with no rooms for shenanigans. After enjoying the steam room, I took a shower in a large communal stall. As I came out of the shower and began toweling myself, a handsome young man, about thirty (I was sixty), started a conversation, asking if I was an American. I said I was. He said that he had recently been in the States. I asked where. "Alabama," he replied. "Peter?" I asked. He looked amazed. "How do you know my name?" "You were supposed to visit Edwin and me in Charleston last month." A mutual friend in Alabama had asked us to show Peter around Charleston when he came to stay with the son of that friend. Peter then asked me if there was a place where we could go. I took him to the apartment, learning that he liked older men. He had two permanent ones, one in London and another in Amsterdam.

This meeting was to have wonderful results for us as he introduced Edwin and me to his friends, many of whom would visit us in Charleston or whom we would visit in London or in their summer getaways in the country. Eventually, we seemed to have more gay friends in London than in Charleston, and, with most of them still living, it continues to be that way. We often exchanged visits with Egbert, the Amsterdam friend who was a theater director and actor with a large circle of friends who were dancers, actors, and musicians.

We investigated the purchase of a flat in London but it was too expensive. There were almost always friends with whom to stay before we went off exploring other countries. We went several times to Spain, partly to see my old friend Harold from the "Jeb and Dash" days. He had been dismissed from the State Department after over twenty years of service during the McCarthy era. By going to Madrid to live permanently, he had honed his skills as a painter and was hired by the Spanish Government to restore its national treasures. I asked him once what he was doing when I saw a tiny brush in his hands. "Practicing my Velasquez stroke," he said. Before his death, he was awarded the highest honor given in Spain, one that had never before been given to a foreigner.

We would go with him and his friend, Jesus, to any of the five gay bars still functioning under Franco. I often wondered what the city would have been like under the President before the fascists took over. After an interview once, the President was asked by the reporter if he would excuse a delicate question, "How did you become a homosexual, Mr. President?" Showing no hesitancy, he replied, "By showing curiosity, young man, just as you are now."[1]

Edwin and I enjoyed the ambience of the bars with their music, guitars, voices, and the friendliness of even the young men toward the middle-aged. We went out from Madrid to many interesting cities, villages, and to Morocco once to escape the 106-degree heat in Seville.

An amusing incident occurred when we took the train to Toledo to visit the El Greco museum. A priest was sitting by the window, Edwin next, and me on the aisle. Across from us were two elderly Spanish ladies in black. Edwin had the Paris edition of the *Herald Tribune* spread across his lap, and the priest soon had his hand under the paper and in Edwin's crotch. Edwin, who didn't want to embarrass the priest in front of the women, allowed the touching to go on until we reached Toledo, when the priest removed his hand. As the women left their seats to leave the train, they kissed the priest's hand.

At this museum, like many others we visited over the years, Edwin and I went our separate ways to explore the displays at our own pace. So, I was in a different room when a guard approached Edwin and, as he stood in front of different paintings, would touch Edwin's crotch, pointing with his other hand to the painting and saying, "Muy bueno." Edwin was simply too handsome for people to resist. Throughout the years, we never initiated the sexual encounters but accepted them with a sort of noblesse oblige.

A more mutually agreeable encounter occurred on our first visit to Lisbon. We had arrived early in the morning, so slept in until early afternoon. We left our hotel to search for a restaurant but were faced with something different when a handsome young man, again about thirty, stopped us. He began talking in good English and told us that he was on his country's soccer team and had just returned from a victory in England. He wasted no time in asking us if we would take him to our hotel room. What better introduction to this beautiful city, where other splendid attributes were enjoyed for the next ten days? I think we had more curiosity than lust, always wanting to find out what made people tick, whether they were generous or self-serving, genuine or false.

A thwarted encounter occurred in Leningrad when we were there with Bob and Edward. When we returned from a ballet performance, Edwin and I decided to stop at the bar for a beer. Next to us was an attractive young man who said he was a student at the university, from Saigon. When he went to pay his bill, the bartender couldn't change his note so we offered to pay. However, he said that he had had several beers and wouldn't let us pay. When he left, we moved to a table. A few minutes later, he returned with two handsome Russian students and asked if they could sit with us. We chatted for more than an hour, and, knowing that students were not allowed in this hotel, I realized that we were being set up for sexual blackmail. We didn't let on that we suspected and eventually excused ourselves. My suspicions were confirmed the next morning when I saw the student who said he was from Saigon emerge from one of the hotel offices.

Bob and Edward were also with us on a month's visit to Greece, where we rented a car. While in the beautifully situated town of Naplion, we went one afternoon to a famous, well-preserved amphitheater, where we watched a rehearsal of a play as the sun set in one direction and the moon began to rise in another. Suddenly, we saw two waiters from our hotel making their way up to the top where we were sitting. They had heard us discuss our plans and had come here on a motorbike.

We left with them, one sitting in the back between Edward and Bob, the other meeting us on his bike at a tavern on the road. We had lamb from a spit and ouzo and soon were watching a number of men form a line and begin a dance. I was urged to join them and did. However, in a few minutes, a bottle crashed at my feet, and I hastily returned to the table. I learned later that this was a form of approbation. Bob and Edward seemed to enjoy the waiter in the car with them, and it was obvious that "our" waiter expected something of us. All he got was a five-dollar bill. Frequently, in Greece, we were given looks that indicated a willingness to be seduced or whatever, but we resisted such advances, even when they came from the Adonises on the beaches.

Just Edwin and I went to Iran, more exotic than any place we had been. We were particularly taken with Shiraz and the ruins of Persepolis. This was the last year of the Shah's reign, and children would come up to us with smiles and gentle "hellos." The Scandinavian countries each had

Figure 14.1 Edwin and John in Europe, circa late 1970s.

their special charm, too. In Copenhagen once we were sitting on a bench in a large square, resting, when a young Korean asked if he could sit with us. "Of course," we said. He told us that he had been brought to Oslo when he was fifteen by a doctor who had been doing charity work in Korea. He was adopted, given a college education, and was now a teacher in Oslo. When he got up to leave, he asked if he could go to our hotel with us. Well, we decided, this would be the closest we would ever get to Korea, and he would be a pleasant introduction to that country from which I would later have many young music-student friends. In a couple of years, we had an invitation to his wedding.

We often visited relatives or friends in the United States and sometimes drove our European friends to the mountains or cities they wanted to visit. They would be amused by Edwin, who would occasionally, at a rest stop, get out of the car and stand on his head or skip rope to keep awake.

In 1978, we were saddened by the death of Bob, who died of an internal injury that was undetected after a fall down his back steps. When Edward discovered Bob's lifeless body beside him in bed in the middle of the night, he went into shock and was admitted to a hospital until he recovered. Edward lived on another ten years. He spent a month with us in a beautiful Hampstead flat we were loaned in London and, in another year, joined me in London while Edwin was touring China with my old friend Bo. I didn't want to go there because of a queasy stomach that made me fearful of Chinese food. We were with Edward in Asheville during most of the last days of an extended illness, in 1988.

Like our other friends who were couples, Edward and Bob had lived without complications because of their sexuality. Our friends lived in their own homes in friendly neighborhoods, never went to psychiatrists, never suffered ostracism. In adolescence they accepted their liking for the same sex without anxiety.

During the years after the war, my literary life was almost at a standstill. I became involved with the Poetry Society again but I never wrote well when I was happy. An occasional poem came out and was published or remained unread in a drawer. In 1984, I had enough verse to make a book, and *Alaska and Beyond* was published. It didn't create any waves, but I liked seeing much of that work from the war years in one place and at least Edwin and our families were pleased.

That summer we were returning from a movie when we heard a voice saying, "Are you looking for a playmate?" We weren't, but we were so astonished by the overture of the handsome youth that we took him home. He was a Charlestonian and a student at the university in Columbia. He was so charming we allowed him to return the next night, after which we never saw him again. My mother had always told me to be kind to strangers, and I usually followed her advice.

On a visit to London in 1987, Edwin went into a bookstore near Covent Garden. He noticed a large picture of Carson on a wall and copies of her books on the shelves. He asked the young manager why there was so much interest in McCullers. He replied that she was the favorite writer of his friend, Noel Virtue, born in New Zealand, whose first novel was about to be published. When Edwin explained his relationship with Carson, it turned out that Noel had just read Virginia Carr's *The Lonely Hunter*, in which Edwin figured prominently. The young man asked if he might bring Noel to the apartment where we were staying, and the next night they appeared, bringing Noel's splendid first book, *The Redemption of Elsdon Bird*. They returned the next evening for supper, and a friendship began which still continues. In his *Once a Brethren Boy* he discusses our meeting.

For its tranquility, beauty, and the universal friendliness of its people, New Zealand became our favorite country. If we had been younger and not had family we loved, we would have considered moving there. Our interest started when we entertained Una, an artist, one of those friends of a friend who often stayed with us. She lived in Takapuna, a small town across the bay from Auckland, and she urged us to make the long journey, with a stop in Sydney, to meet her good friend Berri. We liked Berri at once and, on future visits, stayed with him. Una introduced us to her literary and artist friends, some of whom had cars, and found us the charming Mon Desir motel in a grove of trees sacred to the Maori. We began reading splendid New Zealand writers whom she had known. We traveled the islands by bus, getting off when a town or area seemed interesting. By the time of our second visit, we felt very much at home.

Noel Virtue had not returned at that time, having had fundamentalist parents who had cast him out as a youngster when they caught him performing oral sex on an older brother, who had initiated the act but was not punished. Noel was sent to an institution and passed his home on the way to school but without recognition by his family. When he was in his teens, he found work in Wellington, saved enough money to get to London, where he couldn't find a job. He became a prostitute for a year until he found a job in a zoo. Soon afterward, he began writing. It was only after his parents were dead that he felt able to return to his homeland with his companion from the bookstore. New Zealand was the only country that allowed this. He continued to write many fine books and receive numerous awards until a heart attack, years later, brought his writing career to an end.

My third visit to New Zealand and Australia was with Edwin's sister and her husband on a trip that the four of us had planned before Edwin's death. I had been informed by a young man, met at a party in London and recently working in Shanghai, that he would be in Sydney when we were. We got in touch at his friend's home. I was invited for lunch after which we went back to his bedroom. When I was leaving, he urged me to return to England with him to set up a life together but I hadn't any interest in doing that. I was seventy-eight and who could take the place of Edwin?

Of course, Edwin and I were at home or at the beach most of the year. Edwin became known as "the angel of Wentworth Street," as he swept in front of neighbors' houses, took the elderly to doctors or elsewhere, and was always available when help was needed. We became concerned when an elderly widow who lived three doors down from us hadn't put out her garbage can. There was no answer to our telephone call, so Edwin called the police, who came immediately. They took a big ladder from under our house and put it up to Helen's bedroom window at the back of her house. But the police would not break a window to get in. Edwin broke it, and the police thanked him. Helen was lying on the floor, naked, unconscious, but alive. An ambulance was called, and, after she was able to leave the hospital, we found her a nursing home. By then, her best friend, a legal secretary, had made me Helen's executor. We cleaned her house, had a successful sale of its contents, and then sold it. A cousin had showed no interest in her predicament because she thought she might become financially responsible. I invested Helen's money, paid her bills, and, when she became seriously ill, just before I was leaving for Europe, helped the cousin choose a casket and gown should she die while I was away. She did, and, when I returned, her friend in the lawyer's office brought us her will, leaving almost everything to the Catholic Church. However, the cousin had visited Helen in the hospital later and had her draw up a new will leaving her everything, negating the older will.

In the spring of 1989, on a routine visit to his doctor, Edwin was taken for an overnight stay in a hospital for further tests. It was discovered that he had a serious heart condition, manageable with pills. Edwin underplayed the seriousness of his condition but stopped his early morning bike rides and walks, when he often picked up coins saved for the homeless shelter.

In early August, we drove up to Highlands (sometimes called Fire Highlands) to stay at a pleasant little motel we had discovered on other visits. We saw gay and straight friends who summer there and had a quiet, relaxing time in that charming town. We returned home with the prospect of a vacation in France with one of my nephews and his wife, who were my best friends. Edwin's doctor had said that he could go if he didn't overdo.

On the morning of August 23, 1989, Edwin got up early, made muffins for an overnight guest who was still sleeping, and left me at the kitchen table to go to the Senior Citizens Center, where he went from time to time to have his blood pressure checked. A few minutes later, I had a call from that center, telling me that Edwin had had a heart attack. I aroused our friend, and, when we got to the center, I saw Edwin lying on the floor, his shirt off, his head in a pool of blood where he had fallen. Firemen from across the street were trying to revive him. An ambulance came, and we followed it to the hospital and awaited news from the emergency room. A doctor appeared and told me that Edwin had died.

I was in a state of shock but maintained my composure when I was with others. My way of coping with grief or disappointment will not be everyone's. I have a fairly stoic personality and have always felt gratitude for what has been good in my life. Much of that came from Edwin and knowing how he would have hated life as an invalid, and how many of his pleasures had been curtailed by his heart problem, which I had to take into consideration when dealing with my own loss.

His sister and her husband, whom we had often visited in Phoenix, came, and they, their son and wife and my sister, Virginia, and I drove in two cars with his ashes to Thomasville, where he was buried without any religious ceremony, at his request. His ashes, in a simple cardboard box, were placed in the earth to become part of nature, as he desired. In Thomasville and during our drives, the talk was all about Edwin and what he had meant to each of us.

I received over 200 letters from around the world, most of them from heterosexuals who extended sympathy and extolled Edwin's virtues. One, from a widow in Highlands, said that during the weekend we spent with her she recognized the same bond between us that she had known with her husband.

The next month I went to France as we had planned, and much of our time was talking of the beauties of Edwin rather than of the French countryside. Hurricane Hugo struck while we were away, and I returned to many problems that Edwin would have solved more easily.

122 Book Basement, Travels, and Beyond

Figure 14.2 Edwin looking down onto John, circa 1980s.

With forty-nine years of wonderful memories, I learned to cope with grief. Edwin had always requested that I dry off the ceramic shower walls after a bath, but I always said that, since he would be using the shower afterward, it was a waste of time. Since his death, I dry down those walls every day and have a sort of communion with that rare human being.

For Edwin:

Like some great playful fish of the sea
Or a winged strength cleaving the air
While we moved at a snail's pace on firm earth,
You went through your life, always sure
That water was there to swim through,
Thunderstorms never to be evaded, a test
Only of wings that were given at birth.
In the stillness that has fallen over us,
Although we have lost a focus for our vision,
There stirs in the emptiness a breath fighting
To become a life worthy of that gift
Bestowed as freely as the sun's warmth
Or the benign beauty of the rising moon.

Afterword
After Edwin

"I am alone. I have always dreaded loneliness...."
Diary entry of John Zeigler, Jr., February 2, 1938

When Edwin passed from John's life, there was a void. John missed Edwin terribly, but outwardly he was stoic. The couple was together for nearly half a century. The two had become one while each maintained his individuality. There would be other opportunities for John to live with another, like the young man who wanted to "set up a life together" in London, but this had little appeal. Loneliness, however, was not a welcomed choice either.

In the two decades that I have known John, he has never been alone for very long and has remained intellectually and physically active. Each week he reads several books, mostly literary biographies, novels, letters, diaries, and poetry. There always seems to be a trip planned or one just completed, and the house, which he calls "Slipshod Manor," is seldom empty for too long as friends or caring relatives frequently visit. Music has always been an important aspect of John's life, and, in his later years, he became a patron of the arts, supporting the music program and its students at the College of Charleston.

As the sole surviving member of the Washington group of gay men, chronicled in *Jeb and Dash*, John sometimes receives letters from interested readers who have tracked him down through the Internet. One such person, Michael Conley, spoke often with John as he wrote and produced a play based on Carter Beeler's edited diary. More inquiries come, however, from John's knowledge about Carson McCullers and the close friendship that he and Edwin had with the novelist. More often than not, these inquirers—researchers, journalists, documentary filmmakers—lead to other friendships.

It was when John lived in Washington, D.C., that he decided to become a writer. Although the children's book he wrote in Alaska and the novel he wrote later have never been published, nor have his plays been performed, many of his poems have been published. Two books of John's

Figure 15.1 John with actor John Clayton portraying him in a play by Michael Conley based on the book *Jeb and Dash*, 2005.

poetry were also released. *Alaska and Beyond* was a compilation of poems written mostly during World War II that had appeared earlier in publications, such as the *American Mercury, Harper's Bazaar, Good Housekeeping, New York Times,* and *Washington Post.* A more personal collection of poetry, *The Edwin Poems,* compiled many previously unpublished poems written during the couple's forty-nine-year relationship and after Edwin's death.[1]

Like Carter, John kept a diary during his time in Washington. Although not as lengthy as Carter's voluminous entries, John's more poetically written diary gives insight into another gay man's life during the Depression.[2] It reveals the character of a twenty-five-year-old bored with his bureaucratic day job and struggling to find his true calling, troubled by a relationship of convenience while yearning for a true love, disgusted by his "crowd of belittlers, gossips, backbiters" yet fearing loneliness.[3]

In late autumn of 1937, John wrote in his diary:

> It rains incessantly. This is one of those rare nights when I am alone and can choose from everything near to me in the room that which suits the moment. How each moment changes! The eyes tired of reading, the mind desires the solace of music, or the hands feel the magnetism of the pencils that stand in the little orange jar that once held a cactus and lent its color and life to the mantel in that large, unfriendly room I had on Twentieth Street.
>
> Earlier this evening I was reading a life of Rimbaud by Enid Starkie and earlier in the week I read Nicholson's life of Verlaine. What tempests their lives were. Rimbaud insatiable, Verlaine intensely human and, therefore, to me, more tragic. There is something more terrible in the man beset with the small evils, the qualities of laziness, cowardice, inertia, the man who, having almost everything, appears to the outside world in the degradation of being slave to his incapabilities, than in any larger canvas of passions haughty and grandiose with evil that is incarnate and all consuming, terrible and yet so resplendent with this terribleness that it invokes a sympathetic awe more than anything else. How quiet my life seems, the life of a good clerk. . . .
>
> I have desired love which would consume me utterly and I have destroyed the possibility of its appearance by succumbing to a passion which had much of the ignoble and unhealthy in it. It rains violently against the roof and drops fall down the chimney. How good to be alone—and yet tomorrow I will surely desire companionship.[4]

John's relationship with Bo during those Washington days was physically enjoyable but emotionally unsatisfactory. He was fond of Bo but not in love with him. "I don't like to receive affection I cannot honestly return," he penned in his diary. Yet, "rather than hurt him I pretend to feel that which I do not."⁵ When John returned to Charleston, in the early spring of 1940, the relationship between the two ended. That July, he finally met the man he had imagined in his diary two years earlier: "I could be happy with a friend to share the dreams I have of the days when I have enough money to enable me to retire and live at the beach...."⁶

After Edwin and John sold The Book Basement and retired in 1971, there was indeed more time on the beach as well as many trips overseas. But, their life together—like so many other older couples, be they gay or straight—largely centered around the ordinary: games of bridge with friends like Kip and Jerry; Edwin's morning walks where he would often find loose change which he gathered to donate to the Interfaith Crisis Ministry; reunions with Edwin's or John's families; John baking sugar cookies or making quantities of fig and pear preserves; Edwin puttering in his garden or raking leaves dropped from the huge pear tree; John's afternoon visits to his mother's home, where she lived with her sister. That normalcy ended on a muggy morning in late August, 1989.

After Edwin's death, John's thoughts turned to ways in which he might contribute to his memory and further support the arts in Charleston. He began supporting the College's music program. He first established the Edwin Davis Peacock Scholarship for Strings, Edwin having played the violin before he was ten. While his mother was still alive, John endowed a piano scholarship in her name, followed by an award for piano performance in his sister Virginia's name. Over the years, John also established

Figure 15.2 Edwin and John at couple's screened porch, October 1972, Charleston.

nine scholarships or gift annuities with the College Foundation. He arranges for a talented music student to stay in the dependency behind his house rent-free each year. In return, the student helps him with errands and cares for the garden. "The rewards for me have been significant," he told a writer for the Foundation's newsletter. "The students get something but I also get something. . . . "[7]

Among the young people who have benefited from John's generosity and who shared some of their lives with him are opera singer José Lemos and pianist Florencia di Concilio. Lemos has already established himself on the world's stage, and di Concilio composes music for television and films in France.

Surrounded by friends and family, books and music, John is seldom alone or lonely. The pensive youth writing into his diary seventy years ago is not unlike the man today approaching the century mark, with the exception that he found "the one necessary friend."[8] And with that special person he realized life's most important lesson. "Being in love," observed the Russian dramatist Anton Chekhov, "shows a person who he should be." Edwin and John showed that to one another—and together they share that with us.

Notes

Introduction

1. I. Russell (Ed.) (1993) *Jeb and Dash: A Diary of a Gay Life, 1918–1945*, Boston, Mass.: Faber & Faber.
2. J. Sears (1991) *Growing Up in the South: Race, Gender, and Journeys of the Spirit*, Binghamton, N.Y.: Haworth Press; J. Sears (1997) *Lonely Hunters: An Oral History of Lesbian and Gay Southern Life, 1948–1968*, New York: Harper Collins/Westview; J. Sears (2001) *Rebels, Rubyfruit, and Rhinestones: Queering Space in the Stonewall South*, New Brunswick, N.J.: Rutgers University Press; J. Sears (2006) *Behind the Mask of the Mattachine: The Hal Call Chronicles and the Early Movement for Homosexual Emancipation*, Binghamton, N.Y.: Haworth Press.
3. J. Sears (1997) Race, Class, Gender and Sexuality in Pre-Stonewall Charleston: Perspectives on the Gordon Langley Hall Affair. In J. Howard (Ed.), *Carryin' On: An Anthology of Southern Lesbian and Gay History* (pp. 164–200), New York: New York University Press; J. Sears and L. Allen (2000) Museums, Friends, and Lovers in the New South: Laura's Web, 1909–31. *Journal of Homosexuality*, 40 (1): 105–44; L. Allen and J. Sears (2003) Laura Bragg and Her "Bright Young Things": Fostering Change and Social Reform at the Charleston Museum. In J. Hutchisson and H. Greene (Eds.), *Perspectives on the Charleston Renaissance* (pp. 155–75), Athens, Ga.: University of Georgia Press.
4. Sears, *Behind the Mask of the Mattachine*, p. 10.
5. C. McCullers (1951) *The Ballad of the Sad Café and Other Works*, Boston, Mass.: Houghton Mifflin, p. 27.

1 Clingman's Dome

1. I. Russell (Ed.) (1993) *Jeb and Dash: A Diary of a Gay Life, 1918–1945*, Boston, Mass.: Faber & Faber.
2. C. McCullers (1940) *The Heart is a Lonely Hunter*, New York: Houghton Mifflin, p. 1.
3. Several of these individuals were homosexual. For the definitive biography of Bragg, see L. Allen (2001) *A Bluestocking in Charleston: The Life and Career of Laura Bragg*, Columbia, S.C.: University of South Carolina Press. For details of the gay artist Ned Jennings, and Bragg's support of him and other homosexual artists and writers, see J. Sears and L. Allen (2000) Museums, Friends, and Lovers in the New South: Laura's Web, 1909–31. *Journal of Homosexuality*, 40 (1): 105–44.

2 A Cure?

1 The play, cowritten by Jane Cowl and Jane Murfin (under the nom de plume of Allen Langdon Martin), starred Cowl. In 1922, it was made into a silent picture featuring the great actress Norma Talmadge, and then, eight years later, into a "talkie." In 1932, it went to Broadway as an operetta, *Through the Years*, with the only successful part of the production being the title song.
2 Published in 1910, Mme. La Marquise de Fontenoy's work was one of many such efforts that gave an eager reading public an insider's look into various European courts, ranging from fashion to personal anecdotes. Despite its "tell-all" quality, heterosexual intimacies were simply alluded to, and homosexual liaisons and scandals, such as the 1907 Harden–Eulenburg Affair, were omitted. For details, see J. Steakley (1990) Iconography of a Scandal: Political Cartoons and the Eulenburg Affair in Wilhelmin Germany. In M. Duberman, M. Vicinus, and G. Chauncey, Jr. (Eds.), *Hidden from History: Reclaiming the Gay and Lesbian Past* (pp. 233–57), New York: Meridian.
3 See J. Zeigler (1925) *The Last of the Bighams* (Orangeburg, S.C.: Sandlapper, 1984); K. Boling (1984) *A Piece of the Fox's Hide*, Orangeburg, S.C.: Sandlapper.
4 For more details on the early life of Carson McCullers, see V. Carr (1975) *The Lonely Hunter*, Garden City, N.Y.: Doubleday; B. Clark and M. Friedman (Eds.) (1996) *Critical Essays on Carson McCullers*, New York: Hall; J. Savigneau (2001) *Carson McCullers: A Life*, Boston, Mass.: Houghton.

3 What Must One Do?

1 C. Willingham (1947) *End as a Man*, New York: Vanguard Press. Twenty-four-year-old Calder Willingham's first novel read "like the notes of a small-town peeper on the broom closet of hell" (Adolescent's Daydream, *Time*, March 13, 1950). Although obscenity charges were lodged twice against his publisher, the result was acquittal for this critically acclaimed and popular novel. Willingham, a native Southerner, then wrote the theatrical adaptation, which appeared as an off-Broadway production in 1953 (James Dean played a small role in the Actors Studio workshop version). Willingham later penned the 1957 screenplay, *The Strange One*, which was released with newcomer Ben Gazzara playing the role as Sergeant Jocko De Paris. Due to film codes of the era and the story's homosexuality, a female character was inserted while the homosexual cadet, Perrin McKee, appeared as the repulsive "Cockroach," played by Paul Richards. Additionally, three minutes of the film's more troublesome footage was edited out. For more information, see A. Slide (2003) *Lost Gay Novels*, Binghamton, N.Y.: Haworth Press.
2 D. Heyward (1925) *Porgy*, New York: George Doran Company. For detail on Porgy (actually Goat Cart Sam), the development of the novel, and its author, see http://xroads.virginia.edu/~hyper/porgy/porgy.html; see also D. Bostick and D. Crooks (2005) *On the Eve of the Charleston Renaissance: The George W. Johnson Photographs*, Charleston, S.C.: Joggling Board Press; J. Hutchisson (2000) *Dubose Heyward: A Charleston Gentleman and the World of Porgy and Bess*, Jackson, Miss.: University Press of Mississippi.
3 Later, after John graduated, the magazine expanded to include some advertisements (one for Camel cigarettes featured the homosexual actor Montgomery Clift). Besides contributions from cadets, others who were published in *The Shako* included John Bennett and Herbert Ravenel Sass.

Interestingly, the editor who succeeded Zeigler, William Geer, was also a gay man who later became a North Carolina professor. An audiotape interview with Geer about his experiences at The Citadel as a homosexual cadet can be found in the Sears Papers, Special Collections Library, Duke University.

4 For details about the Charleston Renaissance, see H. Greene (2001) *Mr. Skylark: John Bennett and the Charleston Renaissance*, Athens, Ga.: University of Georgia Press; J. Hutchisson and H. Greene (Eds.) (2003) *Renaissance in Charleston: Art and Life in the Carolina Low Country, 1900–1940*, Athens, Ga.: University of Georgia Press; M. Severens (1998) *The Charleston Renaissance*, Spartanburg, S.C.: Saraland Press.

4 The Incident

1 Key West would not become the enclave for gay men until the 1970s, but there were certainly gay men living in this isolated town prior to World War II. Tennessee Williams, who would later call Key West his home, first arrived two months after Edwin and John's visit. "There are comparatively few tourists and the town is real stuff," he wrote a friend. "Homes are mostly clapboard shanties which have weathered gray with nets drying on the front porches with great flaming bushes of poinsettia in the yards" (L. Leverich [1995] *Tom: The Unknown Tennessee Williams*, New York: Crown, p. 399). On the heels of his failed play, *Battle of Angels*, one of Williams' first stops was Sloppy Joe's bar, the former hangout of Papa Hemingway. (In the early 1960s, it was known as "The Olde Bar," the first gay-friendly bar in the town.) Living in the former slave quarters of the old Trade Winds mansion, Williams periodically banged out poems on his typewriter with *Leaves of Grass* by his side.

2 Well before World War II, New Orleans enjoyed a reputation for gay life. There was the red-light district, known as Storyville, a no-holds-barred enclave that dated from the 1880s until World War I and included Emma Johnson's Basin Street studio, where lewd shows were performed every night, and Miss Carol, whose establishment of Baronne Street housed boy whores with interracial entertainment. Less noticeable were the exclusive social groups, included Mardi Gras krewes, some of which were largely composed of gay men. For heterosexual tourists, gay life was evident in "femme mimics" shows found at the Wonder Bar on Lake Pochetrain and later at the famous My-O-My Club with its three nightly shows which listed male names beneath female photographs. Mr. Gene Lamar sang arias. As a female soprano, he sometimes stopped in the middle of "Ritorna vincitor," from *Aida*, to tell the audience, in his rugged voice, "Don't worry, I'll make it." And, for gay men in the know, there were long-standing bars such as Café Lafitte and the legendary Dixie's bar of Music, run by Miss Dixie Fasnacht and her sister Miss Irma. See J. Sears (2001) *Rebels, Rubyfruit, and Rhinestones*, New Brunswick, N.J.: Rutgers University Press.

3 Letter to John Zeigler from George S., June 14, 1941. Copies of all letters are located in the James T. Sears Papers, Perkins Library, Duke University.

4 Letter to George S. from John Zeigler, June 14, 1941.

5 Letter to George S. from John Zeigler, August 7, 1941.

5 Lean Wolf Hours

1 There was an extensive set of novels with gay or lesbian characters or themes published or available in the U.S.A. during the 1920s and 1930s. Although many of these characters were tragic, e.g., *The Butterfly Man* (1934), odiously

depicted or camouflaged (the female pronoun is used throughout the 1932 novel, *A Scarlet Pansy*), this often was done to avoid censorship. There, too, were posthumously published novels, such as E. M. Forster's *Maurice* (1971). Nevertheless, a surprising number—such as *Better Angel* (1933), *The Young and the Evil* (1933), and *Strange Brother* (1931) were remarkably positive. With a few notorious exceptions, such as the often-banned *Well of Loneliness* (1928), widespread publicity about this genre of fiction, however, did not occur until after World War II, notably with the publications of Truman Capote (*Other Voices, Other Rooms*), Gore Vidal (*City and the Pillar*), Patricia Highsmith (*Strangers on a Train*), and Carson McCullers (*The Heart is a Lonely Hunter*). For more information, see R. Austen (1977) *Playing the Game: The Homosexual Novel in America*, Indianapolis, Ind.: Bobbs-Merrill; J. Foster (1956) *Sex Variant Women in Literature*, New York: Vantage; B. Grier (1981) *The Lesbian in Literature: A Bibliography*, 3rd edn, Tallahassee, Fla.: Naiad Press; J. Levin (1983) *The Gay Novel: The Male Homosexual Image in America*, New York: Irvington; M. Lilly (1993) *Gay Men's Literature in the Twentieth Century*, New York: New York University Press; S. Malinowski (Ed.) (1994) *Gay and Lesbian Literature*, Detroit, Mich.: St. James Press; J. Rule (1975) *Lesbian Images*, New York: Doubleday; G. Sarotte (1978) *Like a Brother: Male Homosexuality in the American Novel and Theatre from Herman Melville to James Baldwin*, New York: Doubleday; A. Slide (2003) *Lost Gay Novels: A Reference Guide to Fifty Works from the First Half of the Twentieth Century*, New York: Harrington Park Press; C. Summer (1990) *Gay Fictions, Wilde to Stonewall: Studies in a Male Homosexual Literary Tradition*, New York: Continuum; G. Woods (1998) *A History of the Gay Male Literature Tradition*, New Haven, Conn.: Yale University Press.

2 The WPA was established by the Roosevelt Administration in 1935 to provide employment to persons in every state in the Union. It became the largest single employer in the country as workers engaged in projects from constructing public buildings and roads to operating artistic projects, such as the writing workshop in which John participated.

3 Ina Russell's heavily edited version of her uncle Carter's fifty volumes of diaries, introduces "Nicky Bowman," her pseudonym for John, in an entry dated June 18, 1931. John is described as having a "soft accent of the native Washingtonian." In a later entry (October 31, 1931), reported by Russell, "Nicky" has an automobile, had attempted suicide in the springtime, and "had become a close friend of a wealthy manufacturer, and the wife of the manufacturer sued for divorce on account of Nicky." John was a native Carolinian, an upperclassmen at The Citadel in 1931–2, never attempted suicide, and did not own an automobile during his stay in Washington (1934–40).

Correcting these and other inaccuracies, Zeigler excused the discrepancies, observing: "When Ina Russell edited the diaries of her uncle, Carter, she was faced with the daunting task of condensing thousands of pages into one volume. She was also concerned about keeping anonymity of the persons talked about in the diaries. This led her to some changes which, unfortunately, in my case was to have me die while I was in the Navy, thus showing that a gay man gave his life for his country. Happily, that was untrue and when the diaries were published I was the only one in the rather closed-knit group still living."

In *Jeb and Dash*, Russell explains that "a great deal of material needed to be left out. . . . For the sake of coherence, causal acquaintances were cut altogether and a few of the characters were given the task of bearing events

132 *Notes*

belonging to more than one person. . . . Certain other changes seemed essential. The sheer size of Jeb's diaries demanded fusing details" (I. Russell [1993] *Jeb and Dash*, Boston, Mass.: Faber & Faber, pp. 3–5). The historical record has been corrected for "Nicky."

6 A Yeoman's Journey

1 By the early 1940s, bars which catered to a homosexual clientele included the Brass Rail, Pirate's Cave, the Silver Rail, the Black Cat, and the Silver Dollar. However, San Francisco's homosexual past extends at least as far back as the Barbary Coast era, with homosexuals working out of Turkish baths and the infamous Dash saloon, opening in 1908, featuring female impersonators and an easy rendezvous for quick sex (N. Boyd [2003] *Wide Open Town*, Berkeley, Calif.: University of California Press, p. 25). There, too, were the South of Market Boys, a group of young professional and mostly homosexual men who formed a social-service group following the great earthquake and fire in 1906 (J. Sears [2006] *Behind the Mask of the Mattachine*, Binghamton, N.Y.: Haworth Press, p. 232).

2 Finocchio's was opened as a speakeasy during Prohibition, but its infamous floor show did not become widely known until after Prohibition's end and its move from Stockton Street to Broadway following a 1936 police raid (Boyd, *Wide Open Town*, p. 53). Before Finocchio's, Tati's Café hosted Rae Bourbon and his "Boys Will be Girls" production—which was raided in the early 1930s (J. Loughery [1998] *The Other Side of Silence*, New York: Henry Holt, pp. 58–9). For a description of the "pick-up scene" at Finocchio's in the 1930s by post-war gay activist Harry Hay, see: http://www.archive.org/search.php?query=collection%3A%22ephemera%22%20AND%20(subject%3A%22Harry%20Hay%22)%20AND%20subject%3A%22Finocchio's%22 (accessed October 4, 2008).

3 For historical details about the role of gay men serving in World War II and how homosexuality was largely ignored by military leaders during most of the conflict, see M. Berube (1990) *Coming Out Under Fire*, New York: Free Press; T. Carrington and E. Yeates (1996) *Stars Without Garters: Gay G.I.s in World War II*, San Francisco, Calif.: Alamo Square Press; J. Costello (1985) *Virtue Under Fire*, Boston, Mass.: Little Brown, pp. 101–19; Loughery, *The Other Side of Silence*, pp. 135–57.

7 Colorado Schooling

1 *Swann's Way* is the first of seven books comprising Proust's semi-autobiographical *In Search of Lost Time*, written between 1913 and 1927. The gay novelist's concern about the meaning of love and time, as understood through an unnamed narrator's memories, is especially relevant to Edwin and John's story.

8 Yakutat

1 Letter to Edwin, January 31, 1943.
2 Letter to Edwin, March 27, 1944.
3 Letter to Edwin, March 27, 1944.
4 Letter to Edwin, March 27, 1944.
5 Letter to Edwin, April 3, 1944.
6 During World War I, Maugham did hospital work for the British Red Cross in a unit informally known as the "Literary Ambulance Drivers." It

included e. e. cummings, John Dos Passos, Ernest Hemingway, and Desmond MacCarthy. While serving in Flanders, Maugham met twenty-two-year-old Frederick Haxton, who would become Maugham's lover and secretary for the next thirty years; Maugham married in 1917 but was divorced ten years later. In his autobiographical 1915 novel, *Of Human Bondage*, Maugham wrote: "The important thing was to love rather than to be loved." In late 1940, Maugham moved to Parker's Ferry, South Carolina (about fifty-five miles south of Charleston). He lived in a three-bedroom, Carolina pine-paneled, white clapboard cottage, built for Maugham by his publisher, Nelson Doubleday, who owned the 200-acre Bonny Hall Plantation on the Combahee River. There he completed his mystical bestselling novel, *The Razor's Edge*. (T. Morgan [1980] *Maugham: A Biography*, New York: Simon & Schuster; S. Rogal [1997] *A Somerset Maugham Encyclopedia*, Westport, Conn.: Greenwood.)
7 Letter to Edwin, December 29, 1943.
8 Letter to Edwin, March 15, 1943.
9 Letter to Edwin, June 5, 1943.
10 Letter to Edwin, March 21, 1943.
11 Letter to Edwin, May 13, 1943.
12 W. Lewis (1944) *Fighting Words: Stories and Cartoons by Members of the Armed Forces of America*, Philadelphia, Pa.: Lippincott, pp. 28–37.
13 Letter to Edwin, January 6, 1944.
14 For a discussion of Glasgow's work and life, including her close female friendships, both in her novels' characters and in real life, see P. Matthews (1994) *Ellen Glasgow and a Woman's Traditions*, Charlottesville, Va.: University of Virginia Press.
15 "Elegy XIII," *Poems of John Donne*, Vol II, 1896, ed. by E. Chambers, New York: Scribner's, p. 130.
16 Letter to Edwin, March 2, 1944.
17 Letter to Edwin, March 27, 1944.
18 Letter to Edwin, June 19, 1944.

9 Cape Chiniak

1 Letter to John from Edwin, March 8, 1943.
2 Letter to John from Edwin, May 22, 1943.
3 Letter to John from Edwin, n.d., 1943.
4 Letter to John from Edwin, January 25, 1943.
5 Letter to John from Edwin, April 12, 1943.
6 Letter to John from Edwin, August 11, 1943.
7 Letter to John from Edwin, April 17, 1943.
8 Letter to John from Edwin, April 17, 1943.
9 Letter to John from Edwin, June 11, 1943.
10 Letter to John from Edwin, July 22, 1943.
11 Letter to John from Edwin, December 1, 1943.
12 Letter to John from Edwin, March 2, 1944.
13 Letter to John from Edwin, January 6, 1944.
14 Letter to John from Edwin, February 2, 1944.
15 Letter to John from Edwin, January 27, 1944.
16 Letter to John from Edwin, January 24, 1944.
17 Letter to John from Edwin, February 27, 1943.
18 Letter to John from Edwin, April 12, 1943.
19 Letter to Edwin from George Scheirer, February 13, 1943.
20 Letter to John from Edwin, February 11, 1944.

134 *Notes*

21 Letter to George S., from Edwin, October 4, 1943. See also Letter to John from Edwin, September 13, 1943.
22 Letter to John from Edwin, June 11, 1943.
23 Letter to John from Edwin, July 5, 1943.
24 Letter to John from Edwin, July 5, 1943.
25 Letter to John from Edwin, June 15, 1943.
26 Letter to John from Edwin, June 11, 1943.
27 Letter to John from Edwin, June 22, 1943.
28 Letter to John from Edwin, May 24, 1943.
29 Letter to John from Edwin, July 5, 1943.
30 Letter to John from Edwin, May 24, 1943.
31 Letter to John from Edwin, August 25, 1943.
32 Letter to John from Edwin, January 27, 1944.
33 Letter to John from Edwin, July 22, 1943.
34 Letter to John from Edwin, August 11, 1943.
35 Letter to John from Edwin, July 14, 1943.
36 Letter to John from Edwin, September 28, 1943.
37 Letter to John from Edwin, September 28, 1943.
38 Letter to John from Edwin, October 3, 1943.
39 Letter to John from Edwin, October 3, 1943.
40 Letter to John from Edwin, June 11, 1943.
41 Letter to John from Edwin, August 11, 1943.
42 Letter to John from Edwin, October 18, 1943.
43 Letter to John from Edwin, n.d. (circa November, 1943).
44 Letter to John from Edwin, November 11, 1943.
45 Letter to John from Edwin, January 1, 1944.
46 Letter to John from Edwin, March 21, 1944.
47 Letter to John from Edwin, March 30, 1944.
48 Letter to John from Edwin, April, 1944.
49 Letter to John from Edwin, June 7, 1944.

10 Reunion

1 Letter to Edwin from John, July 3, 1944.
2 Letter to Edwin from John, July 4, 1944.
3 Letter to Edwin from John, July 4, 1944.
4 Letter to Edwin from John, July 8, 1944.
5 Letter to John from George S., June 25, 1944.
6 Letter to Edwin from George S., May 19, 1944.
7 Letter to Edwin from George S., June 11, 1944.
8 Diary of Carter Beeler, July 20, 1944. Since "Nicky" had already been killed in Ina Russell's edited version, there is no entry for this gathering in her published book. A typed copy of this diary entry, provided by John Zeigler, is located in the Sears Papers.
9 Letter to Edwin from George S., July 28, 1944.
10 Letter to Edwin from John, July 27, 1944.
11 Letter to Edwin from John, July 27, 1944. Chicago's gay community, including its bars, existed well before World War II. During the 1920s, some lesbians and gay men congregated in the near-northside Bohemian neighborhood known as Towertown. Aptly named for the presence of Chicago's old gray stone water tower, "the last remaining landmark of the sternly moral, overgrown village that was Chicago before the fire becomes the symbol of the bizarre and eccentric divergencies of behavior which are the color of bohemia. . . . Most of Towertown's present population are egocentric poseurs,

neurotics, rebels against the conventions of Main Street or the gossip of the foreign community, seekers of atmosphere, dabblers in the occult, dilettantes in the arts, or parties to drab lapses from a moral code which the city has not yet destroyed" (H. Zorbaugh [1929] *The Gold Coast and the Slum: A Sociological Study of Chicago's Near North Side*, Chicago, Ill.: University of Chicago Press, pp. 87, 92). While some gay men of this era enjoyed the Chicago Opera and the nearby Art Institute, activist Henry Gerber organized the briefly lived Society for Human Rights (J. Sears [2006] *Behind the Mask of the Mattachine*, Binghamton, N.Y.: Haworth Press, pp. 44–5). The gay subculture expanded throughout the 1930s (D. Johnson [1997] The Kids of Fairytown: Gay Male Culture on Chicago's Near North Side in the 1930s. In B. Beemyn (Ed.), *Creating a Place for Ourselves: Lesbian, Gay, and Bisexual Community Histories*, New York: Routledge, pp. 97–118). During World War II, mixed clubs, such as the Capitol Lounge on State Street (where the subway had just been opened in the autumn of 1943), catered to GIs who streamed in by the thousands on weekend leave.
12 Letter to John from George S., July 27, 1944.

11 Edwin's Discharge

1 Letter to George S. from John, September, 1944.
2 Letter to John from George S., September 27, 1944.
3 Letter to John from George S., October 8, 1944.
4 Letter to George S. from John, October 23, 1944.
5 McCrea is best known for his Westerns effused with male bonding, most notably *Ride the High Country* (where he paired up with the homosexual legendary actor Randolph Scott). The six-foot-three-inch blue-eyed McCrea, however, co-starred in the 1932 RKO film, *The Sports Parade*, featuring him as a champion wrestler, Sandy Brown. Again, male bonding was integral to the film, which originally included one song with the lyric "a bisexual built for two," to be sung by Sandy to his best friend from Dartmouth, Johnny Baker (William Gargan). Although this never made it into filming and, on the surface, the plot centered around two men in love with the same girl, it actually gravitated around "two love affairs. . . . One of [which] is between the McCrea and Gargan characters. The other involves the camera's love for Joel McCrea's physique. . . ." In one scene, viewers watch as McCrea wrestles in very tight white briefs with the camera settling on "a conventionally stereotypical pair of pansies who can't take the man-on-man violence. One waves a disdainful hand and says to the other, 'Oh God. This is just brutal. Let's go.' Both are slender, youngish, with wavy hair and pale skin, physically the antithesis of McCrea and Gargan characters." The film includes nude locker scenes with the two slapping towels and wrestling. (R. Barrios [2002] *Screened Out: Playing Gay in Hollywood from Edison to Stonewall*, New York: Routledge, p. 78.)
6 Memorandum to Executive Officer from Edwin Peacock, December 9, 1944 with officer's response on backside. Sears Papers.
7 Laguna Beach would become one location for the 1952–3 evening discussion groups on gay-related issues and would play a pivotal role in the founding of the Mattachine Society. An early Mattachine activist, Gerry Brissette recalled, "Laguna Beach was a community of gays . . . the mayor was gay, the sheriff was gay, and the librarian was gay. They just seemed to be running everything and they were very wealthy." Interview with Gerard Brissette by John D'Emillio, November 1, 1976. El Cerrito, Calif. Tape 00429. International Gay Information Center Collection, Special Collections, New

136 *Notes*

York Public Library. For details on early gay organizing in Southern California, see J. D'Emillio (1983) *Sexual Politics, Sexual Communities*, Chicago, Ill.: University of Chicago Press; J. Sears (2006) *Behind the Mask of the Mattachine*, Binghamton, N.Y.: Haworth Press.
8   Letter to Edwin from John, March 1, 1945.
9   Letter to Edwin from John, March 17, 1945.
10 Letter to Edwin from George S., February 7, 1945.
11 Letter to Edwin from George S., February 22, 1945. For detail about Washington, D.C. gay life before and during World War II, see D. Johnson (2004) *The Lavender Scare*, Chicago, Ill.: University of Chicago Press, pp. 43–55.
12 Letter to Edwin from John, March 25, 1945.
13 Letter to John from George S., August 10, 1945.
14 Letter to John from George S., April 14, 1945.
15 Letter to John from George S., May 9, 1945.
16 Letter to Edwin from John, April 21, 1945.
17 Letter to John from George S., June 4, 1945.

12 At Sea

1   *The Marriage of Heaven and Hell*, Proverbs of Hell (Plate 7).
2   Letter to George S. from John, November 29, 1944.
3   Letter to Edwin from George S., January 25, 1945. See original letter to John from George S., January 3, 1945.
4   In this 1945 novel, banned in fourteen states and three million copies sold, Kathleen Winsor chronicles the heroic actress Amber St. Clare's sexual frolics through Restoration England. It was released as an Otto Preminger film in 1947.
5   Letter to Edwin from John, March 20, 1945. (Emeralds on the Home Front [August 10, 2002], *The Guardian*, Book Review.)
6   Letter to Edwin from John, March 25, 1945.
7   Letter to Edwin from John, March 25, 1945.
8   Letter to Edwin from John, April 25, 1945.
9   Letter to Edwin from John, May 13, 1945.
10 Letter to John from George S., July 1, 1945. Six weeks later, George wrote John (August 27) that Stuart had dropped in "the other night with a big Buick car from his home in New Jersey," accompanied by his roommate, Paul, who appeared to be doing well despite his dismissal. Near the end of 1945, John learned that Stuart's boyfriend, Paul, had "fought it tooth and nail, with witnesses, doctors, and psychiatrists, with the net result that the entire file has been marked 'closed' by a special conciliation board, and by a unanimous vote. He feels vindicated and happy." (Letter to John from George S., circa November, 1945.)
11 Letter to George S. from John, July 11, 1945.
12 Letter to John from George S., July 15, 1945.
13 Letter to George S. from John, October 24, 1945.
14 Letter to Edwin from George S., circa fall 1945.
15 Letter to John from George S., circa fall 1945.
16 Letter to George S. from John, December 4, 1945.

13 The Book Basement Years

1   Letter to George S. from John, February 22, 1946.
2   Letter to John from George S., February 16, 1946.
3   Phil is fictionalized as Max in the "Jeb and Dash" diary.

4 Many of these persons were gay or bisexual. Prentiss's collaboration with Hughes was particularly noteworthy. Taylor designed the four lithographs, including "Christ in Alabama" and "8 Black Boys," that appeared in *Scottsboro Limited: Four Poems and a Play in Verse* (1932, New York: Golden Stair Press). The paper-bound version was sold widely to raise funds for the infamous Alabama trial. The monthly N.A.A.C.P. magazine, *The Crisis*, also included reproductions of Taylor's work. His extensive correspondence with Hughes and Van Vechten is archived at Beinecke Rare Book and Manuscript Library of Yale University. For more information, see A. Rampersad (1986) *The Life of Langston Hughes: I Too Sing America*, New York: Oxford University Press, pp. 221–41.
5 Letter to George S. from John, March 19, 1946.
6 Although white citizens, most notably Judge J. Waties Waring, played an important role in Charleston, most of the civil-rights work was pursued by black men and women. One of those was Septima Clark, who was dismissed in 1956 from her teaching position because of her refusal to resign from the N.A.A.C.P. Clark helped form citizenship schools for African Americans on Johns and Wadmalaw Islands and also helped organize throughout the South. (S. Clark [1962] *Echo in My Soul*, New York: Dutton.)
7 For more detail, see L. Allen (2000) *A Bluestocking in Charleston*, Columbia, S.C.: University of South Carolina Press.
8 Details regarding pre-Stonewall gay life in Charleston can be found in Sears' taped interviews with Julian "Jerry" Hayes which, along with his correspondence, diaries and photographs, are located in the Sears Papers.
9 For details on the murder and trial, see J. Sears (2001) *Rebels, Rubyfruit, and Rhinestones*, New Brunswick, N.J.: Rutgers University Press, pp. 210, 318, 362 n. 18.
10 Published in 1936 and later made into a Disney animated short film, *Ferdinand the Bull*, it is a tale of a bull who prefers smelling flowers to responding to a matador's provocations. Written at the outset of the Spanish Civil War, it was seen by both sides as an attack on the Franco regime and a statement for pacifism. Because of the book's themes of choosing one's own path, gender transgression, and responding to a bully, it has also been identified as a gay-themed book for younger readers by children's writer Alex Sanchez (http://www.alexsanchez.com/gay_teen_books.htm), GLSEN (Gay, Lesbian, Straight Educators Network), and PlanetOut.
11 Gay life in Batista Cuba is detailed in Marc Vargo's (2003) *Scandal: Infamous Gay Controversies of the Twentieth Century*, Binghamton, N.Y.: Haworth Press, pp. 132–4.
12 When not living in France, Italy or their cottage on the English Channel, during Hall and Troubridge's twenty-eight-year relationship the couple spent much of their time at their flat, located in the fashionable area of Mayfair, near Hyde Park.
13 Letter to John Zeigler from Maurice Sendak, spring 1954.
14 David Heisser (n.d.) *The Book Basement Remembers with Love*, Sears Papers.
15 Letter to John from George S., June 15, 1959.

14 Last Years

1 José Antonio Primo de Rivera, founder of the Falange Española, was alleged to have been homosexual and an acquaintance of the homosexual avant-garde poet and playwright Federico Garcia Lorca (D. Foster [1999] *Spanish Writers on Gay and Lesbian Themes*, Westport, Conn.: Greenwood, p. 15; M. Falcoff [1998] *A Culture of Its Own*, New Brunswick, N.J.: Transaction, p. 107).

Afterword

1. J. Zeigler (1984) *Alaska and Beyond: Selected Poems*, Charleston, S.C.: Tradd Street Press; J. Zeigler (2007) *The Edwin Poems*, Philadelphia, Pa.: Xlibris. One poem appeared in both books but with slightly different titles given the different context; "To Her Sleeping," was changed to "To You Sleeping."
2. One entry for the same date and event confirms the validity of both diaries and the differences in the diarists' voices. In the original diary entry for January 19, 1938, Carter wrote:

> Soon after I got back from Candlestick, about 8:45, Perks and John invited me to go for a walk in the snow. Jack arrived just then so he went too. We had a most pleasant and interesting walk. Up to Q Street Bridge and down the slippery bank to Rock Creek Parkway Drive. The woods were beautiful with the black trees against the white snow. The creek water looked very dark and cold. When we got within sight of the Taft Bridge we came to hundreds of young people coasting on a hill on a track that started beside the Shoreham Hotel. Some were even trying to ski. It was fun to watch them all but my feet were quite cold. We went to the top of the hill. Perks and Jack went to the drugstore for something to eat while John and I watched. We came on home by a bus from Taft Bridge. Quite a jolly little outing altogether. They all came into my living room and we talked and read.

For that same day, John entered into his diary:

> It began snowing at noon and by five o'clock the streets were covered with the fine flakes. How muffled the snow makes all that yesterday was strident and harsh. This is the first of the winter and it seemed to make people happy. There were friendly faces above most of the high collars and many people that I passed seemed to have songs on their lips. I know that I did. I felt so joyous I almost ran, and then I would slow down, and all the time I had that quick, exciting feeling that stirs the heart out of its accustomed pace. I wanted to repeat and repeat, "It's beautiful, it's beautiful," not to convince myself but because there might be someone who was too immersed in his own minor catastrophe to see what might make him forget it if he was told of the white beauty that came quietly and surely on the earth. Tonight after seeing the movie Hurricane I walked through Rock Creek Park with Perks, Carter, and Jack. It was calm and beautiful there, the creek black, and with the running sound of coldness. Many people were riding sleds. It was all festive, friendly and made me feel good.

3. Diary entry, February 2, 1938.
4. Diary entry, November 12, 1937.
5. Diary entry, January 6, 1938.
6. Diary entry, March 9, 1938.
7. Cornerstone, Spring 2007, College of Charleston Foundation, p. 2.
8. Diary entry, February 27, 1938.

Index

Note: References for entries within the notes section are followed by a number in parentheses which refers to the chapter in question

African Americans 87, 104
Aldredge, Bob 77, 79, 85, 103, 117–118

Babin, Victor 21
The Ballad of the Sad Café (novel) xvi
Bankhead, Tallulah 87
Bass, Nell 77, 105
Beeler "Jeb" Carter XX: diary of xv, 3, 77, 79, 131n3(5), 134n8(10); 138n2; friendship with Zeigler 23, 28, 105, 123; personality 29, 52; relationship with Isham "Dash" Perkins 29–30
Bell, "Max" Phil 28, 77, 101
Bennett, John xv, 16, 110, 129n3(3)
Benny, Jack 39
Bergman, Ingrid 56, 59
Bigham, Edmund 9, 10
Bragg, Laura 5, 16, 18, 103–104, 110, 128n3(1)
Brissette, Gerry 135n7(11)
Brown, Dee 25
Burnett, Whit 12
Butwin, Frances Mazo 110
Byrnes, Jimmy 17

Call, Hal xvi
Carr, Virginia 119
Cather, Willa 22, 88
Charleston Renaissance 16
Charleston, SC i, xiii, xv, 5, 8, 14, 16, 17, 19, 21, 24, 31, 36–7, 53, 69, 76–7, 81–2, 85, 94, 97, 101–6, 113, 115, 126, 136n6(13), 136n8(13)
Chekhov, Anton 127
Chicago, IL 79–80, 134n11(10)
City and the Pillar (novel) 106
Citadel xii, 8, 14–16, 106, 110, 130n3(3)
Civil Rights movement 104
Civilian Conservation Corps xiii, 10, 18
Clark, Mrs. Mark 110
Clark, Septima 136n6(13)
Clift, Montgomery 129n3(3)
Coleman, Richard 5
College of Charleston 13, 94, 103, 106, 109–110, 113, 123
Columbus, GA 5, 10
di Concilio, Florencia 127
Conley, Michael 123
Copland, Aaron 102
Cowl, Jane 129n1(2)
The Crisis (magazine) 137n4(13)

Deasy, Jack 35
Death Comes for the Archbishop (novel) 22
Dobbins, Jack 106

End as a Man (novel) 14, 129n1(3)

female impersonators 36, 130n2(4), 132n1(6), 132n2(6)
The Story of Ferdinand (novel) 137n10(13)
Field, Rachel 102
Fighting Words (book) 55

Florence, SC xiii, 9, 17
de Fontenoy, La Marquise 129n2(2)
Forever Amber (novel) 89, 136n4(12)
Friendly Persuasion (novel) 30

Geer, William 130n3(3)
Gerber, Henry 134n11(10)
Glasgow, Ellen 59, 89, 133n14(8)

Halsey, William 5
Hall, Radcliffe 109, 137n12(13)
Hamilton, Neil 56
Harden–Eulenburg Affair 129n2(2)
Hayes, Julian "Jerry" (and Kip) 104–6, 112, 126, 136n8(13)
The Heart is a Lonely Hunter (novel) xiii, xvi, 5, 10, 131n1(5)
Heisser, David 110
Heyward, Dorothy xv, 5, 37
Heyward, DuBose 5, 14, 109
homosexuality: blackmail 117; cinema and 129n1(3), 129n3(3), 135n5(11); and McCarthyism 31, 106, 136n10(12); in military 49, 68, 88, 95, 105, 132n3(6); novels about 14, 26, 130n1(5), 132n1(7), 133n14(8), 137n10(13); scandals regarding 129n2(2); silence around 25
homosexuals: bars and 21, 36, 80, 105, 116, 130n1(4), 132n1(6), 134n11(10); baths 39, 86, 132n1(6); in Cuba 108; in communities 19, 84, 104, 113, 130n1(4), 134n11(10); cruising among 23, 26–27, 80; discrimination 95, 114, 116; friendships among 21–22, 25, 29–30, 95, 103; long term relationships between xv, 50, 88, 104–5, 114, 119; in Mexico, 107; organizing 134n11(10), 135n7(11); sexual relationships among 84; suicide 16, 31; violence against 105–6 *see also* homosexuality
Hughes, Langston 102, 137n4(13)
Hutty, Alfred 16

Isle of Palms, SC 3
Jeb and Dash (book) xv, 3, 123, 131n3(5); *see also* Carter "Jeb" Beeler, Isham "Dash" Perkins

Jennings, Ned 5, 128n3(1)
Johnson, Topie 4, 17, 24, 42, 67

Key West, FL 19–20, 130n1(4)

Lamar, Gene 130n2(4)
The Last of the Bighams (book) 9
Lemos, Jose 127
Lorca, Jose 137n1(14)
Lowell, Amy 16

Manila 94
McCrea, Joel 135n5(11)
McCullers, Carson Smith xii, xv, 10–12, 39, 52, 68, 84, 102–3, 110–112, 123
McCullers, James Reeves 12, 68, 84, 103, 110
Mann, Thomas 20
Marks, Hilda 112
Marks, Robert 112
Mattachine Society xvi, 135n7(11)
Maugham, Somerset 51, 132n6(8)
Mayrant, Drayton 110
Mead, Margaret 95
The Member of the Wedding (novel), 10, 103
Mercer, Mary 112
Mount Pleasant 104
murder cases 9, 10, 105–6
Murfin, Jane 129n1(2)

National Association for the Advancement of Colored People (NAACP) 104, 136n4(13), 137n6(13)
Native Americans 49, 54, 56, 58–9
Newberry, Edward 9, 39, 77, 79, 85, 89, 103, 117–118
New Orleans, LA 130n2(4)

Other Voices, Other Rooms (novel) 106

Peacock, Edwin: in Alaska during WWII 46, 62–75; The Book Basement 14, 37, 82, 93–4, 97–8, 101–111, 114, 126; in Colorado during WWII 43–5; in California during WWII 36, 38–40, 83, 85, 96–7; childhood xiii, ; civil rights 64, ; in Civilian Conservation Corps 10, 18; correspondence to Zeigler 57, 62–75; death 121;

early relationship with Zeigler 3–5, 7, 19, 22–23, 36, 54, 60, 126; family of xiii, 17–18, 35, 80, 98 109; friendships in WWII 64–6, health problems 38, 40, 83–5, 121; hobbies and interests 18, 20, 63–4, 66, 68–9, 70, 72, 85, 106, 126; The Lonely Hunter 119; Carson McCullers and 10–12, 68, 84, 102; James Reeves McCullers and 12; personality 5, 22, 40, 104, 120; in Philadelphia during WWII 84; plans after the war 52–53, 60, 69, 82, 84, 93–94; in Portland during World War II 81–3; post war relationship with Zeigler 106, 108–9; relationship with Zeigler's family 6, 35, 67, 108–9; in Santa Fe, 20–21; sexual experiences 10, 18, 39, 108, 116–119; as Singer in *The Heart is a Lonely Hunter* 5, travel with Zeigler 6–7, 18, 19, 20, 108–9, 116–121; in Washington D.C. during WWII 77, 79, 84–5; World War II service entry 20, 37; World War II serving together with Zeigler during 38–9, 42, 68, 69–70, 81, 96–7

Perkins, "Dash" Isham: friendship with Prentiss Taylor 101; friendship with Zeigler 23, 28, 52, 77; hobbies and interest 29; relationship with Carter "Jeb" Beeler 29–30, 138n2; work at State Department 31; visits to Charleston 105

Philadelphia, PA 84

Pinckney, Josephine xv, 16, 21, 102, 110

Poetry Society of South Carolina 16, 110

Porgy (play) 129n2(3)

Portland, OR 81–2

Pound, Ezra 102

prostitution 96, 119, 130n2(4)

Proust, Marcel 37, 96, 132n1(7)

The Razor's Edge (novel) 133n6(8)

Reconstruction Finance Corporation 3, 17, 25

de Rivera, Jose Antonio Primo 137n1(14)

Russell, Ina xv, 131n3(5)

St. Vincent Millay, Edna 16

San Francisco, CA 36–7, 39, 132n1(6)

Santa Fe, NM 20–21

Sass, Herbert Ravenel 129n3(3)

A Scarlet Pansy (novel) 26

Scheirer, George 25–26, 39; correspondence with Peacock and Zeigler 23–24, 40, 49–51, 67, 76–7, 79–80, 82–5, 88, 95–7, 101–2; 136n10(12); death 112; visit to Charleston 97, 103

Scott, Randolph 135n5(11)

Sears, James i, xi, xv,

The Secret Memoirs of the Courts of Europe (book)

Sendak, Maurice 109

Simons, Katherine 16

South XX; Ku Klux Klan in 9; *see also* Charleston SC, Columbus, GA; Florence SC, Key West, FL, New Orleans, Thomasville, GA, Washington DC

Smilin' Through (play) 8

Smith, Alice Ravenel Huger 16

Smith, Carson *see* McCullers, Carson

Speyer, Leonora 55

Stein, Gertrude 16

Story (magazine) 12

Storyville 130n2(4)

Strange Brother (novel) 26, 129n1(3)

The Strange One (film) 129n1(3)

Sullivan's Island, SC 6, 103, 110, 115

Talmadge, Norma 129n1(2)

Taylor, Prentiss xv, 101–2, 137n4(13)

Thomasville, GA xiii, 10, 11, 17–20, 79, 80, 85, 98, 108, 121

Three O'Clock Dinner (book) 5

Through the Years (play) 129n1(2)

Tucker, Joe 25

Tucker, Mary 12

Van Vechten, Carl 102, 137n4(13)

Verner, Elizabeth O'Neill 16

Virtue, Noel 119–120

Vronsky, Vitya 21

Waring, J. Waties 136n6(13)

Washington, D.C. xv; Dupont Circle cruising 23, 26–28, 84; homosexuals in 29–30, 84, 95

The Well of Loneliness (novel) 26
West, Jessamyn 30
Williams, Tennessee 130n1(4)
Willingham, Caldwell 14, 129n1(3)
Winters, Carol 55–6
Work Progress Administration 26, 131n2(5)
World War II 37, 54, 90, 92; censorship during 49, 51, 68; homosexuals serving in 42, 132n3(6); racial discrimination in 104; USO 55–6, 67 see also Edwin Peacock; John Zeigler

Zeigler, John: in Alaska during WWII 46–61; attitudes about homosexuality 17, 113–114; The Book Basement 14, 37, 82, 93–4, 97–8, 101–111, 114, 126; in Colorado during WWII 43–5; in Boulder during WWII 79–80; in California during WWII 36, 38–40, 86–7, 96–7; childhood xiii, 8–9; Citadel student 8, 38; correspondence to Peacock 49–57, 60–1, 76, 79–80, 83–4, 90–4; correspondence to Scheirer 23–24, 40, 82–3, 87, 95, 97–8, 101; civil rights 104; death of Peacock 121–122; diary of 123, 125, 138n2; early relationship with Peacock 3–5, 7, 19, 22–23, 36, 54, 60, 125; editor of *The Shako* 15, 110, 129n3(3); family of xiii, 8–9, 17, 28, 35, 98, 109; Foothills magazine and 30, 35; friendship with Carter "Jeb" Beeler and Isham "Dash" Perkins 23, 29–30, 52, 105; friendships in WWII 40, 51, 58, 88–9; in Hawaii during WWII 87; health problems 93–95; hobbies and interests 26, 29, 37, 49, 53, 59, 72, 123, 126; in *Jeb and Dash* book 131n3(5), 134n8(10); McCullers and 52; personality 22, 29, 40, 57, 58, 59, 125; as novelist 23, 24, 36, 55, 69, 123; in the Pacific during WWII 81, 86–96; personality 26, 37, 54, 87–8, 92; philanthropy 126–127; plans after the war 52–53, 60, 69, 82, 93–5; as playwright 6, 37, 123; poetry by 3, 7, 8, 13, 16, 19, 31, 47, 86, 106, 119, 122, 125; in Portland during WWII 81; post war relationship with Peacock 106 108–9; publications of 36, 55, 119, 125; in Reconstruction Finance Corporation 17, 25; relationship with Peacock's family 35, 67, 108–9, 120–121; in Santa Fe, 20–21; sexual experiences/relationships 9, 10, 15, 15, 28, 29, 30, 39, 80, 82, 86–7, 89, 108, 116–119; as teacher, 17; travel with Peacock 6–7, 18, 19, 20, 108–9, 116–121; in Washington, DC 17, 25–31, 77, 79, 125; World War II fighting in 90–1; World War II service entry 20, 37; World War II serving together with Peacock during 38–9, 42, 68, 69–70, 81, 96–7